New

CW01647181

Edited by **Gordon Giles** **May–August 2026**

BRF Ministries

15 The Chambers, Vineyard,
Abingdon OX14 3FE
+44 (0)1865 319700 | brf.org.uk

Bible Reading Fellowship is a charity (233280) and company limited by guarantee (301324), registered in England and Wales

EU Authorised Representative: Easy Access System Europe – Mustamäe tee 50, 10621 Tallinn, Estonia, **gpsr.requests@easproject.com**

ISBN 978 1 80039 471 1

Cover photo by pexels.com/@anete-lusina

Distributed in Australia by:
MediaCom Education Inc, PO Box 610, Unley, SA 5061
Tel: 1 800 811 311 | admin@mediacom.org.au

Distributed in New Zealand by:
Scripture Union Wholesale, PO Box 760, Wellington 6140
Tel: 04 385 0421 | suwholesale@clear.net.nz

Acknowledgements
Scripture quotations marked with the following abbreviations are taken from the version shown. Where no abbreviation is given, the quotation is taken from the same version as the headline reference. NRSV: the New Revised Standard Version Updated Edition. Copyright © 2021 National Council of Churches of Christ in the United States of America. Used by permission. All rights reserved worldwide. NIV: The Holy Bible, New International Version, Anglicised edition, copyright © 1979, 1984, 2011 by Biblica. Used by permission of Hodder & Stoughton Publishers, an Hachette UK company. All rights reserved. 'NIV' is a registered trademark of Biblica. UK trademark number 1448790. ESV: The Holy Bible, English Standard Version, published by HarperCollins Publishers, © 2001 Crossway Bibles, a division of Good News Publishers. Used by permission. All rights reserved. KJV: The Authorised Version of the Bible (The King James Bible), the rights in which are vested in the Crown, reproduced by permission of the Crown's Patentee, Cambridge University Press.

The quotation from *The New Testament in Modern English* by J.B. Phillips is copyright © 1960, 1972 J. B. Phillips. Administered by The Archbishops' Council of the Church of England. Used by permission.

A catalogue record for this book is available from the British Library.

Printed and bound in the UK by Zenith Media NP4 0DQ.

Suggestions for using *New Daylight*

Find a regular time and place, if possible, where you can read and pray undisturbed. Before you begin, take time to be still and perhaps use the prayer of BRF Ministries on page 6. Then read the Bible passage slowly (try reading it aloud if you find it overfamiliar), followed by the comment. You can also use *New Daylight* for group study and discussion, if you prefer.

The prayer or point for reflection can be a starting point for your own meditation and prayer. Many people like to keep a journal to record their thoughts about a Bible passage and items for prayer. In *New Daylight* we also note the Sundays and some special festivals from the church calendar, to keep in step with the Christian year.

New Daylight and the Bible

New Daylight contributors use a range of Bible versions, and you will find a list of the versions used opposite. You are welcome to use your own preferred version alongside the passage printed in the notes. This can be particularly helpful if the Bible text has been abridged.

New Daylight affirms that the whole of the Bible is God's revelation to us, and we should read, reflect on, and learn from every part of both Old and New Testaments. Usually the printed comment presents a straightforward 'thought for the day', but sometimes it may also raise questions rather than simply providing answers, as we wrestle with some of the more difficult passages of scripture.

New Daylight is also available in a deluxe edition (larger format). Visit your local Christian bookshop or BRF's online shop **brfresources.org.uk**. To obtain an audio version for the blind or partially sighted, contact Torch Trust for the Blind, Torch House, Torch Way, Northampton Road, Market Harborough LE16 9HL; **+44 (0)1858 438260**; **info@torchtrust.org**.

Comment on *New Daylight*

To send feedback, please email **enquiries@brf.org.uk**, phone **+44 (0)1865 319700**, or write to the address shown opposite.

Writers in this issue

Clare Hayns is a vicar in Oxford, having previously been College Chaplain at Christ Church, Oxford. She has published two books with BRF Ministries – *Unveiled* and *Garden Song* – illustrated with paintings by her artist son, Micah.

Tim Heaton is a parish priest, rural dean, and non-residentiary canon of Salisbury Cathedral. He is the author of the best-selling Lent course *The Long Road to Heaven* (Circle Books, 2013).

Richard Martin worked in insurance before serving with the Church Army in Halifax, Dewsbury, and Strood. He also worked as an RE teacher. After ordination, he ministered in Gravesend and Gloucester.

Barbara Mosse is a writer and retired priest with chaplaincy experience in prison, university, community mental health, and hospital settings. She has led retreats and quiet days and lectured in theological education.

David Runcorn is an Anglican priest, an author, a spiritual director, and a retreat leader. His ministry has included local churches, Lee Abbey chaplain and a director of ordinands. You can meet him at **davidruncorn.com**.

Elizabeth Rundle is a Methodist minister. She has led church weekends and quiet days, broadcast on local television and radio, and published many Bible studies and devotional books.

Margaret Silf is an ecumenical Christian committed to working across and beyond traditional divisions. She is the author of a number of books for 21st-century spiritual pilgrims and a retreat facilitator.

David Walker is Bishop of Manchester. He chairs the United Society, Partners in the Gospel, and is a regular broadcaster on BBC Radio 4, including on *Thought for the Day*, *Prayer for the Day*, and the *Daily Service*.

Veronica Zundel is an Oxford graduate, writer, and columnist. She lives with her husband and son in north London. Her book *Everything I Know about God, I've Learned from Being a Parent* was published by BRF in 2013.

Gordon Giles writes...

It is often said that you cannot put a value on friendship – it is priceless. I am sure this is true, but not long ago a group of students decided that they would try, and discovered, perhaps to their dismay, that the value of friendship is £22.

This they learned not after writing pages of dense text or yards of impossibly complex equations, but rather after a little experiment in marketing. Using eBay, they decided to sell the friendship of Big John, as they called him, who unwittingly had his friendship auctioned online. The person who offered the highest price became the proud, if not bemused, owner of Big John's friendship for exactly a year.

We speak of 'having' friends, and I think that there is an important sense in which we 'own' our friends and they own us. Our ownership consists in the sharing of experiences. Sharing is a kind of mutual owning, for what we share in friendship we jointly own. In that sense we are members not only of the Bible Reading Fellowship (the legal name of BRF Ministries), but of the Bible Reading *Friendship*. Friendships occur among like-minded people, among those with common interests or experiences. Friends care for and about one another, sometimes across vast distances.

We rejoice with our friends, not only because friendship is a gift from God exemplified in Christ, but also because, as Ralph Waldo Emerson put it: 'A friend may well be reckoned the masterpiece of nature.'

One of the chief characteristics of friendship is openness and vulnerability. Jesus called his disciples friends (John 15:15), and they shared his pain as well as his joy. Jesus tells them they are not servants, but friends. They are the first welcomed members of the Christian family – a family which, like all families, has its ups and downs.

The language of possession is also appropriate when we turn to God. We are possessed, in love, by God. In turn, God is ours – ours to love or deny, worship or reject. Yet at the heart of it all is the irreversible truth that God is ours and we are his. We belong to each other – us and God. And we belong among Christ's family of Christians. The basis of that belonging is love. And the chief symptom of love is friendship.

So we give thanks, above all, for each other. Friendship is a gift. By it we are blessed in one another.

GORDON GILES

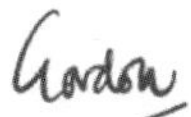

The prayer of BRF Ministries

Faithful God,
thank you for growing BRF Ministries
from small beginnings
into the worldwide family it is today.
We rejoice as young and old
discover you through your word
and grow daily in faith and love.
Keep us humble in your service,
ambitious for your glory,
and open to new opportunities.
For your name's sake,
Amen.

'It is such a joy to be part of this amazing project'

As part of our BRF Resources ministry, we're raising funds to give away copies of Bible reading notes and other resources to those who aren't able to access them any other way, working with food banks and chaplaincy services, in prisons, hospitals, and care homes.

'This very generous gift will be hugely appreciated, and truly bless each recipient… Bless you for your kindness.'

'We would like to send our enormous thanks to all involved. Your generosity will have a significant impact and will help us to continue to provide support to local people in crisis, and for this we cannot thank you enough.'

If you've enjoyed and benefited from our resources, would you consider paying it forward to enable others to do so too?

Make a gift at **brf.org.uk/donate**

The multicolours of scripture

The Bible is written in black and white – dark ink on a pale surface, reproduced throughout the centuries, from parchment to screens, a set of texts presented as scripts. Sometimes it is interpreted in black and white, too – a monochrome either/or, a rule book of dos and don'ts.

Yet even monochrome has shades of grey, and the human eye can distinguish around 500 of them. When it comes to colours, the range increases significantly: we can distinguish up to ten million colours. Individual ability varies, colour-blindness and age-related eye conditions notwithstanding, yet the range of colours discernible by those of maximum discrimination is staggering. Such is the polychromatic beauty of God's creation. Some creatures can discern colours we cannot see – some insects, for example, can 'see' ultraviolet – while others have lesser ocular function.

A spectrophotometer can determine the colour of something in terms of light absorbed and reflected off a surface, but in daily life most of us can recognise and describe colour without much thought. Who knows whether the red I see is identical to what you see, yet we can agree that the fire engine is red nevertheless. By the same token we can safely assume that colours have not changed over the centuries. Thus when we read in the Bible that something is red, amber, green, or black, the colour it conjures up in our mind's eye is fundamentally the same.

There are some colourful characters in the Bible and some Technicolor stories. Some of these have been made into excellent films, biblical epics based on Noah, Moses, Joseph, David, Samson, Daniel, Esther, and of course Jesus and his disciples. Colours are mentioned in the Bible, as in life, by way of illustration. We are told that the robe Jesus is made to wear when he appears before Pilate is purple because it *was* purple, but also because it has meaning, being regal. So where we find colours mentioned in the Bible, they can add authenticity, emphasise a significance, or both.

As we shine a theological spectrophotometer onto some extracts from the black-and-white book that is the Bible, we realise how colourful it is, literally and metaphorically. Turn its pages with me, and let us see what we can see.

GORDON GILES

Brown

Joseph, being seventeen years old, was shepherding the flock with his brothers; he was a helper to the sons of Bilhah and Zilpah, his father's wives; and Joseph brought a bad report of them to their father. Now Israel loved Joseph more than any other of his children because he was the son of his old age, and he made him an ornamented robe. But when his brothers saw that their father loved him more than all his brothers, they hated him, and could not speak peaceably to him.

Combining witty parodies of popular musical genres with punchy, rhyming lyrics, in *Joseph and the Amazing Technicolor Dreamcoat* Andrew Lloyd Webber and Tim Rice created a memorable retelling of this story which has cemented a myth in the popular imagination. Some Bible translations do say Joseph's coat had many colours, but more recent scholarship prefers to say it had long sleeves. It was not as multicoloured as the musical suggests; rather it was likely mainly brown.

But the coat was nonetheless special. It was a gift, perhaps embellished or ornate, perhaps made of different animal hides or fabrics, and it betokened singular, loving favour. It was this favouritism, not the colours, which riled Joseph's half-siblings.

Yet Joseph himself is a multicoloured character. He is sold into slavery, then resold, then taken advantage of sexually by someone with power, who shames him on rejection. He is unjustly imprisoned, but gains freedom by demonstrating a special gift for oneiromancy (interpreting dreams prophetically), and rises to great power and influence through skill, charm, and effort.

Joseph's robe reveals the risks of favouritism. Jacob should have known better, because his father Isaac had favoured Esau over him, but instead of breaking the cycle, he repeats history. Joseph did not choose his fancy coat and was probably obliged to wear it rather than offend his foolishly indulgent father. Jacob's role in this story is one of its subtler, darker colours, because it is his loving but ill-judged action that sets in motion a rollercoaster sequence of events for his favourite son, which brought disaster before success.

Reflect on actions which have caused harm to others, however well meant. Is reconciliation needed?

GORDON GILES

Rainbow coloured

I have set my bow in the clouds, and it shall be a sign of the covenant between me and the earth. When I bring clouds over the earth and the bow is seen in the clouds, I will remember my covenant that is between me and you and every living creature of all flesh, and the waters shall never again become a flood to destroy all flesh.

Joseph's robe may not have been technicoloured, but God's 'bow on the clouds' is. A rainbow is an arc showing red and violet on the outer and inner sides, with other colours appearing in between. Isaac Newton identified the sevenfold sequence of red, orange, yellow, green, blue, indigo, and violet, remembered by many in the mnemonic 'Richard Of York Gave Battle In Vain' (a statement which is also historically true). Caused by light being refracted, reflected, and then refracted again when leaving a drop of water, a rainbow is a meteorological phenomenon usually associated with rainfall and sunlight.

Sirach wrote: 'Look at the rainbow and praise him who made it; it is exceedingly beautiful in its brightness. It encircles the sky with its glorious arc; the hands of the Most High have stretched it out' (43:11–12). In Revelation an angel is crowned with a rainbow (10:1) and around the heavenly throne is 'a rainbow that looks like an emerald' (4:3).

The 'bow in the clouds' is constant; rainbows will always occur and will always look the same. As such they symbolise an eternal hope, an unchanging promise of mutual faithfulness: a covenant. As sure as rainbows are in the sky, so sure is God.

Being colourful, rainbows are associated with positivity, and they have been used as a symbol for all sorts of causes. When South Africa became democratic, Nelson Mandela and Desmond Tutu hailed it as a 'rainbow nation'. The Pride movement deploys rainbows widely. During the Covid pandemic, rainbows were associated with key workers. Hope, diversity, gratitude, promise, joy, and affirmation have all displayed rainbow colours and will continue to do so. For whose heart is not lifted on seeing a rainbow?

What does a rainbow signify to you?
Give thanks to God for it and be joyful.

GORDON GILES

Purple

And they clothed him in a purple cloak, and after twisting some thorns into a crown they put it on him. And they began saluting him, 'Hail, King of the Jews!' They struck his head with a reed, spat upon him, and knelt down in homage to him. After mocking him, they stripped him of the purple cloak and put his own clothes on him. Then they led him out to crucify him.

The robe that the soldiers made Jesus wear when mocking him is one of the most colourful parts of the Passiontide story. If asked, most people would say it was purple, but it should be noted that in Matthew it is scarlet (27:28) and in Luke, the colour is unspecified, but likely white (23:11). Mark and John (19:2) say it is purple. Known as Tyrian purple, because it came from Tyre in Lebanon, the dye was very expensive, as it was manually extracted from rock snails and 12,000 snails were needed to get 1.4 grams of dye. Being a reddish-purple colour, it is understandable how gospel writers might disagree. Indeed, the darker red it was, the more it was prized. It was a labour-intensive, smelly, and lengthy process, but the result was luxurious.

In Acts 16:14, Paul meets a woman, Lydia, who is described as 'a dealer in purple cloth' and therefore presumably rather rich. The valuable purple dye was prized by Romans, who used it in ceremonial robes. That Jesus was publicly but briefly enrobed in it before crucifixion not only mocked any kingship claimed by or attributed to him, but also sent a warning to any Jews contemplating insurrection.

The humiliation of the purple robe is one of various physical and psychological attacks made on Jesus on his final day. As it happens, the dye, while normally obtained by crushing the molluscs, is also secreted by them when hunting prey and released when antagonised. So there is a tragic parallel to this when we consider the stress and abuse Jesus was enduring, reflected metaphorically in the purple robe he briefly wore. As Proverbs puts it: 'Heartache crushes the spirit' (15:13b, NIV).

Reflect on how the way people are treated can damage their mental health. Pray for all those crushed in this way.

GORDON GILES

Crimson red

She puts her hands to the distaff, and her hands hold the spindle. She opens her hand to the poor, and reaches out her hands to the needy. She is not afraid for her household when it snows, for all her household are clothed in crimson. She makes herself coverings; her clothing is fine linen and purple. Her husband is known in the city gates, taking his seat among the elders of the land.

As noted yesterday, according to Matthew's gospel, the robe Jesus is given to wear before his crucifixion is not purple, but scarlet. We also noted that the rich colour of the kingly robe may be described as red or purple depending on the observer's use of language. Red is the colour of blood, and the most-prized Tyrian purple colouring was deep and dark like black-tinted, clotted blood. Purples are blends of red and blue, so the hue varies according to the mix and intensity. Think of the shirts which bishops wear: they range from maroon to an almost blue colour. Ask any bishop what happens when the shirt has been worn and washed many times. In ancient times the colour was renowned for being colour fast, but then it did not have to contend with today's washing machines!

The 'virtuous wife' of Proverbs 31 may be considered contentious in some circles, but we notice her today not because of washing or cooking, but because of her wealth and status, which is deducible from her ability to clothe her household in crimson and purple linen. Only rich people could do that. For some she is the personification of wisdom, so often feminised in the Bible, and so, dressing herself in red and/or purple is a sign of royalty.

Thus she is dressed in strength. To be wise is to be strong and regal; wisdom is the crown of virtues. For some this account is not about a woman at all, but about the regal nature of wisdom. Wisdom is therefore purple, and crimson its natural relation. To have wisdom in one's life is to be richly blessed, like a king or queen. To be clothed in red or purple is to be richly robed with wisdom.

Has wisdom changed over the ages? Do wise people have status today or are those who rule us strong sinners?

GORDON GILES

Black

I am black and beautiful, O daughters of Jerusalem, like the tents of Kedar, like the curtains of Solomon. Do not gaze at me because I am dark, because the sun has gazed on me... Tell me, you whom my soul loves, where you pasture your flock, where you make it lie down at noon; for why should I be like one who is veiled beside the flocks of your companions?... His head is the finest gold; his locks are wavy, black as a raven. His eyes are like doves beside springs of water, bathed in milk, fitly set.

Black is not strictly a colour; rather it is the hue that absorbs all light or denotes its absence. Since the Roman period it has been used solemnly for death and mourning. Many wear black at funerals or, because of its sombre connotations, they are asked not to, where celebration of life is preferred.

Black is the colour of evil – *ater* ('black' in Latin) is the word from which we get 'atrocity'. Yet songwriter Sydney Carter turned Good Friday into Black Friday when he made us sing, 'I danced on a Friday when the sky turned black' – deftly describing the sombre day we call 'good'. The ambiguity of biblical black is a fascinating and provocative phenomenon. Casting light on it illuminates a paradoxical colour that is not a colour, a passive negativity that is full of energy and mystery.

In medieval times Benedictine monks wore black habits as a sign of humility and penitence, but Bernard of Clairvaux accused them of wearing the devil's colour. His Cistercians wore white for purity; by implication black meant the opposite.

The cultural resonances of black are strong. Yet it was one of the first colours used in art and has at various times been very fashionable. In the Song of Songs, traditionally associated with King Solomon, the woman's beauty is grounded in her dark skin, and her lover's raven-black hair is luscious: not sombre, but sensuous, positive, and attractive.

Of all the colours mentioned in the Bible, black is perhaps the one which, as it absorbs light, also absorbs whatever interpretation we wish to imbue it with. So let us be open to its varied and even positive potential.

God, in whom there is no darkness,
help us see you in everything. Amen.

GORDON GILES

White

Then I saw heaven opened, and there was a white horse! Its rider is called Faithful and True, and in righteousness he judges and makes war. His eyes are like a flame of fire, and on his head are many diadems, and he has a name inscribed that no one knows but himself. He is clothed in a robe dipped in blood, and his name is called The Word of God. And the armies of heaven, wearing fine linen, white and pure, were following him on white horses. From his mouth comes a sharp sword with which to strike down the nations, and he will rule them with a sceptre of iron; he will tread the wine press of the fury of the wrath of God the Almighty.

From the Bible, western culture has gained the idea that white symbolises purity. In Christian cultures, brides and first Communion and confirmation candidates wear white. It is the liturgical colour of birth at Christmas, of baptism, and of Easter resurrection. Thus many clergy wear white for funerals nowadays. The black robes of mourning have been replaced with the white robes of hope. Some cultures do not interpret white in this way; in China, for example, red is for marriage and white for death.

However, the New Testament gives us the white robe of Jesus' transfiguration, the white-clad angels at the tomb, and the white horse in Revelation, where we also find white-robed saints, whose robes become white when washed in the blood of the Lamb (Revelation 7:14; see also 6:11). White is the colour of heaven, and it is the colour of Christ. This is Christ's heavenly horse who rides in, a steed steered by faith and truth, a judge leading a white-robed army into the battle against injustice and sin. It is a vivid, terrifying image, as the King of kings rides in to defeat Satan and bring in the new heaven and the new earth.

It is a ferocious and far cry from the gentle 'whiter than white' idea of purity that we have now. We have softened our whites just as we have softened our faith. The harsh realities of martyrdom, judgement, and the fear of God have been turned into white-robed babies at the font and brides walking down the aisle.

Are you worthy of a white robe? How might you become so?

GORDON GILES

Blue

When the camp is to set out, Aaron and his sons shall go in and take down the screening curtain and cover the ark of the covenant with it; then they shall put on it a covering of fine leather, and spread over that a cloth all of blue and put its poles in place... They shall take a blue cloth and cover the lampstand for the light, with its lamps, its snuffers, its trays, and all the vessels for oil with which it is supplied... Over the golden altar they shall spread a blue cloth and cover it with a covering of fine leather and put its poles in place.

The sky appears blue because blue light has a shorter wavelength, scattering better in all directions heavenward. As the colour of the sky, some associate it with higher consciousness or divinity, and as the seas reflect the sky, blue can represent the infinite vastness of the universe. Blue is the colour of wonder.

In Judaism blue represents divine authority and holiness, as we see in the opulent use of blue for the tabernacle and temple decorations. The instruction to use blue for the ark of the covenant can also remind us of a call to obedience to God's law. In Christian art Mary is often depicted wearing blue, because of an association not only with obedience to God, but also with purity and royalty. In Catholic tradition, Mary is the 'queen of heaven' – blue in blue. Because she is the *theotokos*, the 'bearer of the incarnate Word', she can also be thought of as the new ark of the new covenant. The old covenant, or testament, is the law; the new covenant, or testament, is Jesus. Thus both are associated, covered even, with blue.

However, in popular culture 'the blues' can refer to a musical genre or the state of being sad. Two centuries ago the term 'blue devils' was used to describe the hallucinatory effects of severe alcohol withdrawal. Evolving to describe depressed and distressed states of mind, the genre of melancholic songs took on the colour. This sad cultural development diverts from a more ancient positivity about blue.

Creator God, who in vast blueness gave us life and light, inspire obedience in us, that we may joyfully worship Jesus Christ our Lord. Amen.

GORDON GILES

Green

And he said to them, 'How many loaves have you? Go and see.' When they had found out, they said, 'Five, and two fish.' Then he ordered them to get all the people to sit down in groups on the green grass. So they sat down in groups of hundreds and of fifties. Taking the five loaves and the two fish, he looked up to heaven and blessed and broke the loaves and gave them to his disciples to set before the people, and he divided the two fish among them all. And all ate and were filled.

Nowadays things are 'green' if they aspire to the world's greening: the ecological salvation of our planet. The colourful adjective has gained a moral, and sometimes a political, hue, referencing issues about climate change, global warming, and energy.

In the Bible green is the colour of new life, flourishing, and most importantly spring. It is the colour of abundance, fertility, and hope. We recall the green pastures of Psalm 23 or perhaps Cecil Frances Alexander's 'green hill far away', where Jesus died to save us all. Yet in the story of the feeding of the 5,000 we barely notice the passing reference to green grass.

Why are we told the grass was green? Perhaps simply because it was. It dates the story, too: springtime. Rain and the grass it greens are annual, seasonal events. In John's version of the story, he mentions the imminent Passover, a celebration of liberation from Egyptian slavery which connects to the Roman regime in Palestine which many considered to be oppressive. Is this crowd of hungry people, who have fed on Jesus' godly words, a crowd who might rebel against the Romans with Jesus as a kind of second Moses who would lead them to freedom?

The 'people' were men (*andres*) grouped together, a hungry army in the making. Jesus feeds them, grouped like troops in hundreds and fifties. Then he disperses them to prevent rather than inspire a revolt. He would rather teach and feed with the word of God amid the peace and promise of green pastures.

God, whose green grass calls us to work for the flourishing of all creation,
renew in us justice and hope that this earth may yield enough
to feed all your people, in body and soul. Amen.

GORDON GILES

Grey

Listen to me, O house of Jacob, all the remnant of the house of Israel, who have been borne by me from your birth, carried from the womb; even to your old age I am he; even when you turn grey I will carry you. I have made, and I will bear; I will carry and will save.

A 'silver surfer' is an older person who browses the internet, shops online, and uses social media. Online the over-50s are a growing demographic, contributing significantly to the economy. Nowadays everyone expects to live beyond their 50s, perhaps becoming silver-haired in the process. In Isaiah's time average life expectancy capped at about 40, for even while some did live out the 'four score years and ten', infant mortality, disease, and war took their toll. At the time of Jesus, average life expectancy was about 35.

Thus the word 'even' is significant: 'Even if you live long (which you cannot expect to), I will carry and save you', says the Lord. The 'remnant' have endured and survived the slings and arrows of ancient Palestinian life and death, and more specifically the exile imposed upon them by the Babylonians. The release from captivity in Babylon is akin to the Exodus led by Moses. This exile is reckoned to have lasted 70 years – a human lifetime. Thus there would be very few – if any – who returned as the remnant any time after 538BC. Whether or not they are grey-haired, God's covenant with his people endures from generation to generation. References to grey hair remind us of this long-lived promise (see Luke 21:18).

Grey might be considered a boring, dull colour: few people say it is their favourite! It sits between the extremes of white and black, where optimism and pessimism meet. It is the colour of balance, of wisdom. Here in Isaiah it is the colour of patience and constancy. Going grey is a fact of life, a natural phenomenon which may be resisted, but not prevented. Jesus said: 'Do not swear by your head, for you cannot make one hair white or black' (Matthew 5:36). Symbolising the constant love of God, greyness is to be embraced, welcomed, even worn as a badge of honour.

Reflect on your past and future life and how, no matter your age, God has carried you and will carry you still.

GORDON GILES

The game of faith: 1 and 2 Peter

The epistles known as 1 and 2 Peter were sent to churches in what is now Turkey. Peter was in 'Babylon' (Rome) when he wrote the first in about AD64, so we can assume he was there when the second was composed a couple of years later. Some disagreement exists about whether 2 Peter was from his hand, as it is more similar to Jude than to 1 Peter. At this distance we have no way of telling whether someone wrote 2 Peter under the apostle's name, so I will take literally the claim in 1:1 and 3:1 that its author was indeed Simon Peter.

The first letter urges the Christian community not to give up in the face of opposition, to respond with grace to verbal challenges, to maintain high moral standards, and to respect the authorities. The second calls out an invasive, permissive belief system that is threatening their morality and way of living, stressing the importance of their holding on to belief in Jesus' second coming as a motivation for patient holy living.

There is nothing in these letters about mission, church growth, or planning for evangelism. No great plans for serving the community. Nothing about public worship or how to pray. In a sense they are defensive and insular, rather than offering any world-changing agenda. It seems they were written simply with the aim of encouraging the churches to keep hold of the basics of Christian belief and living.

As such, these two epistles call to mind the themes a sports coach might commend to their squad, both new recruits and old hands, at the start of pre-season training. They would not at that stage be focussing on all the games and trophies they hope to win, but rather hone in on the fundamentals and disciplines of the sport, as individuals and as a group – the things to get right from day one if they want the season to go well. In the following reflections, I have imagined this through the lens of football (or soccer), but you could choose another sport if you prefer. Or, if you hate team sports, perhaps instead imagine a staff meeting at the start of a new project or school year.

The challenges Christians faced in the AD60s echo what we face today. We shall be exploring what these letters have to say to us.

RICHARD MARTIN

The coach

This letter is from Peter, an apostle of Jesus Christ. I am writing to God's chosen people who are living as foreigners in the provinces of Pontus, Galatia, Cappadocia, Asia, and Bithynia. God the Father knew you and chose you long ago, and his Spirit has made you holy. As a result, you have obeyed him and have been cleansed by the blood of Jesus Christ. May God give you more and more grace and peace.

If you are a team trainer or coach, you have to have the respect of the team. In football, senior players might say to a new coach, 'Show us your medals.' In other words, by what right do you tell us what to do? Peter has the medals! He had been with Jesus since the earliest days of his ministry, unique in his naming of Jesus as the Messiah, the Son of God, but also in his threefold denial and threefold restoration and as the apostles' spokesman on and after the Day of Pentecost. The churches he writes to can trust that he knows what he is talking about.

When a new minister comes to a church, offering a new insight or style of worship, it is tempting to dismiss him or her as young, naive, or over-ambitious. Let us resolve instead to let them show us their medals – their experience, training, and expertise – and resolve to respect them. In football terms, if our resistance causes them to 'lose the dressing room', the fault is ours, not theirs.

There is another angle to this. Peter, an epistle writer? When Jesus called him, could he read or write? Even if he has dictated these letters, he has come a long way. The football coach may have started his career in the humblest of Sunday league teams or playing boot-less on a dusty patch of ground somewhere abroad. Who could have imagined then where they are now?

So, how do established Christians, well-versed in doctrine and discipleship, view the humanly unpromising members of our church? Those noisy teenagers, that dyslexic adult? Maybe one day they will be Christian leaders. Peter says God knows and chose them.

Dear God, thank you for those who lead and teach in the church now, and for those who well do so in the future. Amen.

RICHARD MARTIN

Life away from the training ground

So prepare your minds for action and exercise self-control. Put all your hope in the gracious salvation that will come to you when Jesus Christ is revealed to the world. So you must live as God's obedient children. Don't slip back into your old ways of living to satisfy your own desires. You didn't know any better then. But now you must be holy in everything you do, just as God who chose you is holy.

Being a serious footballer is a lifestyle choice. It affects what you eat and drink, your sleep pattern, and how you treat your body. Or it should do! Many a famous career has nosedived because of bad influences taking hold. You can do everything right on the training ground, but if you do not live the life when you are at home or with your mates you will not last long in peak condition. A senior player taking a young star under their wing can be crucial.

That is Peter's point here. Those awe-inspiring words 'Be holy in everything you do' are for the churches he is addressing. For them, the temptations that could knock them off course would be about reverting to aspects of their pre-Christian way of living. Self-indulgence in whatever form is the opposite of love for God and neighbour, because love is about self-giving not self-gratification. Whatever they are like in church meetings, they must keep to this new way in the ordinary decisions of life.

There are two aspects of this for long-standing church members. First, new Christians, for whom old friends and lifestyle might still be a powerful draw, need a wise mentor. In advice and prayer, and forgiveness sometimes, could this be you?

Second, what does the call to be 'holy in *everything*' mean for us? Perhaps you can list things you used to do but do no longer, because of your faith. Thanks be to God for those. 'Everything', however, rules out complacency. For example, how holy is our spending and our investment portfolio or pension fund? Are the terms of my will holy? What about our instinctive alignment with shades of politics at home and abroad? Everything? Phew!

Dear God, please show me gently but clearly the next steps in my journey towards holiness. Amen.

RICHARD MARTIN

Team spirit

You were cleansed from your sins when you obeyed the truth, so now you must show sincere love to each other as brothers and sisters. Love each other deeply with all your heart. For you have been born again, but not to a life that will quickly end. Your new life will last forever because it comes from the eternal, living word of God… So get rid of all evil behaviour. Be done with all deceit, hypocrisy, jealousy, and all unkind speech.

The England football players of 1996 were known as the 'golden generation'. Wonderfully talented individuals, starring weekly for their clubs. When they came together for international duty, though, the results were disappointing. Rumours abounded of splits in the camp, groups of players from one club not mixing with those from a rival, and personal grievances from club games creating a bad atmosphere. Did a lack of unity stymie their potential?

Any squad of players will contain old hands and young tyros; people with different pay levels; the extroverts and the loners; those who are popular with the fans, and those who never quite get accepted. A wise coach will include in the training regime a range of activities that nip cliques in the bud and which enhance bonding and unity.

Those who have been members of churches will hear the echoes. Rivalry and power games spoil worship and witness. When I was a child, one Sunday the vicar held up a completed child's jigsaw. 'The church should be like this,' he said, 'showing Christ to the world.' There was a long pause, then he said, 'But this church is like this.' He threw the jigsaw down the aisle and the pieces went everywhere. End of sermon. Silence.

Peter is a wise coach. He knows that without unity the churches he writes to will be churches in name only. He urges them to constantly remind themselves that they are all sinners redeemed by Christ, and to commit to good behaviour towards the others, nurturing love towards each other. That is not always easy, but discipleship is not a journey we make alone.

Dear God, thank you for my Christian sisters and brothers. Help me to love them all. Together let us show Jesus to others. Amen.

RICHARD MARTIN

Are you fit to wear the shirt?

Yes, you who trust him recognise the honour God has given him. But for those who reject him, 'The stone that the builders rejected has now become the cornerstone.' And, 'He is the stone that makes people stumble, the rock that makes them fall.' They stumble because they do not obey God's word, and so they meet the fate that was planned for them. But you are not like that, for you are a chosen people. You are royal priests, a holy nation, God's very own possession. As a result, you can show others the goodness of God, for he called you out of the darkness into his wonderful light.

Peter lists four immense privileges that his readers should never take for granted. Following on from his call to unity, they are aspects of a status they enjoy as a group rather than as individuals.

His readers, Peter says, are, like the people of Israel, chosen by God, belong to God, and a nation devoted to God. Their calling includes both authority and service ('royal priests', following Jesus the servant king). They are like the cosmos in Genesis 1, called out of darkness into light, or like a baby emerged from the womb.

It is as if Peter wants them to look in the mirror and remind themselves of who they are. Humility is a virtue, but imposter syndrome can be powerful, so Peter is asking the church members to see themselves as God sees them, to hear his words of affirmation that remain true however inadequate they may feel.

To put on the kit of a famous club is to enter into its heritage of players who have worn that shirt with distinction in the past or whose feats are part of the club's folklore. To have been chosen to take that heritage forward can feel like a burden and is not to be taken lightly. How many fans would love to wear that kit, even once? If they suspect you are not pulling your weight, they might chant the awful words: 'You're not fit to wear the shirt'.

Dear God, thank you for calling me to be part of your people. Help me to accept the responsibility that comes with privilege. Amen.

RICHARD MARTIN

Never, referee!

For the Lord's sake, submit to all human authority – whether the king as head of state, or the officials he has appointed. For the king has sent them to punish those who do wrong and to honour those who do right… You who are slaves must submit to your masters with all respect. Do what they tell you – not only if they are kind and reasonable, but even if they are cruel. For God is pleased when, conscious of his will, you patiently endure unjust treatment.

Referees make mistakes. Even though dissent is in football a bookable offence, some teams (and managers) have made protest into an art form. To try to prevent such intimidation giving teams an unfair advantage, nowadays video-assisted refereeing (VAR) is in place for big games – but still the decisions are contested! Dissent is beginning to be seen in rugby, too, and even in cricket.

Some clubs, however, have told their players not to protest at a perceived injustice, but to accept the decision and focus on the next passage of play. Getting steamed up about a referee's mistake never gets it changed, and the frustration can adversely affect the team's performance: letting it go is best for you as well as for the referee. The wise coach will instil this attitude long before the first game.

Sadly, corruption and bribery of match officials have been proven on rare occasions. What if the team faces not so much mistakes but deliberate bias? A match where the playing field is far from level? This seems to have been the situation facing Peter's churches. The authorities were not neutral – they were against them and could be cruel. Even in these circumstances, Peter urges a response that rejects complaint and resentment. Twice he uses the word 'submit'. Injustice there may be, but the Christian way is patient endurance.

Sometimes we see court cases in which Christians challenge the decisions of those in authority. They may be our democratic and legal right – but I wonder what Peter would say?

Dear God, you have instilled in humans a sense of fairness. Help me to be Christlike when I or other Christians seem to face injustice. Amen.

RICHARD MARTIN

The dirty tricks they play...

Finally, all of you should be of one mind. Sympathise with each other. Love each other as brothers and sisters. Be tenderhearted, and keep a humble attitude. Don't repay evil for evil. Don't retaliate with insults when people insult you. Instead, pay them back with a blessing. That is what God has called you to do, and he will grant you his blessing.

There is a challenge when the opposing team tries to find ways of getting under your skin, employing tactics designed to make you lose focus. Just as avoiding dissent is key to calm play, so is the refusal to retaliate when the gamesmanship begins. The coach will bring to the team's attention underhand ways opponents might use, such as sly fouls, timewasting, and sledging (a cricket term indicating verbal intimidation or distraction). Inevitably if you do retaliate the referee will spot it and penalise you, rather than the original offender. To keep your head in the face of such provocation is the mark of a dedicated sportsperson – to refuse to stoop to their level but to let your skill shine through.

In the UK, unlike in some countries, Christians face no state persecution. Many, though, know what it is like to be insulted or to have their views rejected. This can go on for years, at home, at work, or socially. It can be exhausting and dispiriting. How tempting to give them a piece of your mind! Peter says that is not the Christian way. Instead, respond by blessing them, and God in turn will bless you.

Being 'fouled' physically or emotionally hurts. What do we do with that pain? We can become hard, and let it bounce off us so others get hurt too. Or we can embrace it and let God transform it in us so goodness flows from us to others and from God to ourselves. It is much easier said than done in the maelstrom of busy, stressful living, and in a culture where becoming offended attracts such attention. Yet the challenge remains. How might I put Peter's teaching into practice today?

Dear God, help me to do your work in your way. Amen.

RICHARD MARTIN

Injuries are part of the game

So then, since Christ suffered physical pain, you must arm yourselves with the same attitude he had, and be ready to suffer, too. For if you have suffered physically for Christ, you have finished with sin. You won't spend the rest of your lives chasing your own desires, but you will be anxious to do the will of God... Dear friends, don't be surprised at the fiery trials you are going through, as if something strange were happening to you. Instead, be very glad – for these trials make you partners with Christ in his suffering, so that you will have the wonderful joy of seeing his glory when it is revealed to all the world.

God's desire for 'shalom', wholeness, and peace for individuals, communities, nations, and the cosmos is at the heart of the gospel. The healing ministry of the church reminds us to believe it even if the healing that ensues is not in the form we had hoped or expected.

The work of The Guild of Health and St Raphael (GoHealth), the Society of Mary and Martha (Sheldon Retreat), and others, helps Christians and churches to see that healing is needed for us, not just for others. Among us there are many who are wounded, perhaps dramatically by a breakdown, loss of faith, bereavement, or relationship closure, but often just worn down and exhausted.

Peter reminds us here that churches are to some extent casualty wards – communities where compassion and space is mutually offered and given, because we are all trying to live out the Lord's Prayer. The petition 'Deliver us from evil' is the last one on our lips. The first is 'Hallowed be your name'. In truly praying this prayer we accept the risk that in putting God first we might become damaged, and we acknowledge the need for healing.

A footballer whose first priority is to avoid injury will not be very committed to the club's glory. Recognising this, modern teams employ experts in physiology and psychology, and create state of the art recuperation programmes and facilities. In showing the depth of God's love, Jesus embraced the pain of the cross. Peter says that in following him we should not be surprised if we get injured.

Dear God, help me to embrace the cross. Amen.

RICHARD MARTIN

Dressing room leaders please note...

And now, a word to you who are elders in the churches. I, too, am an elder and a witness to the sufferings of Christ. And I, too, will share in his glory when he is revealed to the whole world. As a fellow elder, I appeal to you: Care for the flock that God has entrusted to you. Watch over it willingly, not grudgingly – not for what you will get out of it, but because you are eager to serve God. Don't lord it over the people assigned to your care, but lead them by your own good example.

When a minister leaves a church, recruiting a replacement is a tough responsibility. Creating the person specification, job description, or parish profile demands much prayer and wisdom. If you could design your own minister, what skills and qualities would you include? Perhaps words like 'charisma' spring to mind. Not for Peter. The key aspect of ministry for him is genuine caring.

Some of us might baulk at this pastoral model. 'Shepherding' has become a toxic word linked to control and abuse in some contexts. To be 'a sheep' has become an insult, suggesting a loyalty that can slip into dangerous compliance. Yet the biblical metaphor of a shepherd still has great force. Think of the number of times 'The Lord's my shepherd' is sung at funerals. It envisages God as caring for a group and for the individual who strays. The pallium worn by the Pope emphasises this aspect of his role. At times we all give in to cultural norms and behave like a flock of sheep. At times we wander off alone. The shepherd's role even today is to selflessly guide the group and to seek the wanderer.

Every football team has a captain. Some seem to do little more than attend the coin toss and wear an armband. Others, though, can be seen encouraging someone who has made a mistake, urging the team on when they have conceded a goal, or calming them down when they have scored one, receiving and passing on messages from the dug-out, and perhaps taking that crucial penalty in the shoot-out.

We all need leaders who are pastors.

Dear God, thank you for those ministers who care in my setting. Amen.

RICHARD MARTIN

Opponents want to beat us

Stay alert! Watch out for your great enemy, the devil. He prowls around like a roaring lion, looking for someone to devour. Stand firm against him, and be strong in your faith. Remember that your family of believers all over the world is going through the same kind of suffering you are. In his kindness God called you to share in his eternal glory by means of Christ Jesus. So after you have suffered a little while, he will restore, support, and strengthen you, and he will place you on a firm foundation.

A coach will not need to remind serious players of the uncomfortable truth that there are a lot of others who will do their utmost to beat them. 'Each opposing team's coaches will be scrutinising videos of our matches trying to spot our weak points and planning how to exploit them. We need to be alert and never complacent.' Footballers do not spend all their time training among friends. It is in facing opponents that they best hone their skills.

Peter instils a similar mentality in his churches – there is an opposition that will try a range of tactics to unsettle and defeat us. In whatever way we understand the devil, Christians worldwide face opposition in various forms, and it is only by determined resistance and steadfast faith that any of us can endure until life's end.

Nonetheless, we are human and, however much we wish it were not the case, sometimes we give in to temptation. This is part of the suffering to which Peter refers. I find it encouraging that Peter tells us that God will 'restore' us. Perhaps he is thinking of his conversation with Jesus on a beach a few days after the first Easter (see John 21), when he was restored to apostleship. When we fail there is still hope for us too.

In football, it is almost unheard of for a team to be unbeaten in cup and league games throughout a season. At the height of Manchester United's success, their manager Sir Alex Ferguson once said: 'Only true champions come out and show their worth after a defeat.'

Dear God, please give me strength to resist temptation, and faith to believe that you forgive and restore me when I fail. Amen.

RICHARD MARTIN

The daily grind

In view of all this, make every effort to respond to God's promises. Supplement your faith with a generous provision of moral excellence, and moral excellence with knowledge, and knowledge with self-control, and self-control with patient endurance, and patient endurance with godliness, and godliness with brotherly affection, and brotherly affection with love for everyone. The more you grow like this, the more productive and useful you will be in your knowledge of our Lord Jesus Christ.

Turning up to every training session and putting a full effort in will be the baseline of any coach's regard for a player, however talented. The routine of strengthening, endurance, and speed exercises, and the repeated practice of corners, free kicks, and counterattacking can become boring. If you are not picked for the first team week after week, it is easy to lose heart and to slacken your effort. To be in peak condition for the big moments in their career, however, any footballer must constantly work on their fitness.

In this passage, Peter sets out a training regime for church members which will lead them to the full fitness for Christian living which results in practical expressions of love for all. He assumes they all have faith, but that is just the starting point. In the gym of daily life, they have opportunities to bring God's promises to fulfillment by toning up their behaviour, their intellect, their character, and their devotion – learning to love God with more of their body, mind, soul, and strength.

There is nothing spectacular here, no drama. Just a working out of the words of John Keble's hymn 'New every morning is the love': 'If on our daily course our mind be set to hallow all we find, new treasures still of countless price God will provide for sacrifice.' Embracing such growth is part of our response to our prayer 'Give us today our daily bread.'

A good coach will vary the training pattern to make it interesting. Peter's steps from faith into useful love are probably to be thought of more as a spiral than as a straight staircase.

Dear God, thank you for being my wise coach who gives me the training regime I need to grow each day. Amen.

RICHARD MARTIN

The glory days

For we were not making up clever stories when we told you about the powerful coming of our Lord Jesus Christ. We saw his majestic splendor with our own eyes when he received honor and glory from God the Father. The voice from the majestic glory of God said to him, 'This is my dearly loved Son, who brings me great joy.' We ourselves heard that voice from heaven when we were with him on the holy mountain.

Peter could never forget what he saw and heard on the mount of transfiguration. Many Christians can look back to moments of intense spiritual emotion or insight, when the veil between our normal reality and the reality of God's realm is parted. They are times of great blessing, made possible only by the grace of God.

Remember that Peter only had this wonderful experience once. We make a mistake if we expect to live mountaintop spirituality as a norm, because we will find the normal things of life unfulfilling and will feel our prayer life to be not deep enough. So why remember them at all?

In any football club headquarters there will be a trophy room. Here the cups the team has won in the past will be displayed along with photos of famous players, teams, and managers. There may be a few video clips of significant goals, signed shirts, and match programmes, too.

At the start of a season, a coach might lead players new and old on a tour of this space. The point is to instil in them the sense of being part of something bigger than themselves and to encourage them to be caught up in the glory that they share, even if their own exploits do not eventually reach such levels. This year's team might not win a trophy. Yet here is something to which it is worth giving your full commitment.

In remembering the transfiguration, Peter realises afresh why he continues to spend his life in Jesus' cause. Our own spiritual highs may never be repeated, but they inspire us to dedicated service.

Dear God, thank you for granting me a glimpse of your glory. Let me remember clearly and so be motivated to serve you today. Amen.

RICHARD MARTIN

Other voices

But there were also false prophets in Israel, just as there will be false teachers among you. They will cleverly teach destructive heresies and even deny the Master who bought them. In this way, they will bring sudden destruction on themselves... They promise freedom, but they themselves are slaves of sin and corruption. For you are a slave to whatever controls you. And when people escape from the wickedness of the world by knowing our Lord and Saviour Jesus Christ and then get tangled up and enslaved by sin again, they are worse off than before.

Any footballer needs encouragement. Messages of support and admiration are always appreciated. Sadly, these days postings on social media are often negative, hyper-critical, and destructive. Some are brazenly sexist or racist (think of the abuse some players receive after a big game). Others may even have had death threats for the 'crime' of missing a penalty!

The Christians to whom Peter is writing are being subjected to harmful voices. People offering an easy alternative to the disciplined way of Christ-like living have infiltrated the churches and are trying to break down individuals' dedication to Christ.

We must be careful here. One person's understanding of heresy might well be another's recognition of a truth into which the Holy Spirit is gently leading us. We need wisdom and grace so we do not reject new ideas just because they are new. Yet damaging teaching has plagued the church since its earliest days. In recent years survivors of financial exploitation and of physical and sexual abuse in churches have bravely come forward. The root cause of their pain is often other people putting bad theology – heresy – into action.

A wise coach might advise a player to close their social media accounts. Yet there will still be criticism from journalists in the press. Christians too can never shut out the noise that twists for its own purposes God's good news of love for all. Let us be on the alert for any teaching that uses God to justify an attitude to others that is based on or results in anything other than love.

Dear God, please guide in truth and wisdom those whose voices are influential in the church today. Amen.

RICHARD MARTIN

Success may be delayed

Most importantly, I want to remind you that in the last days scoffers will come, mocking the truth and following their own desires. They will say, 'What happened to the promise that Jesus is coming again? From before the times of our ancestors, everything has remained the same since the world was first created'... But you must not forget this one thing, dear friends: A day is like a thousand years to the Lord, and a thousand years is like a day.

As the start of the season draws closer, the coach will begin to explain to the players the way the team will play. This will include the formation and the tactics and the favoured players for different positions, together with those who will be used as impact players from the substitute's bench. All of this might be new to the squad, and there will be sceptics about how it will all work out.

The coach will say that bedding all this in may not yield instant success. Meanwhile the players need to trust the coach's judgement, work hard at the new system, and wait for it to bear fruit.

Peter's churches had probably been told they were in 'the last days', living out a short-term, interim ethic. How long was this going to continue? Was this tough Christian lifestyle based on a mistake? The sceptics were not far away.

Perhaps the question about whether Jesus really was going to return is even more acute among Christians today, some 2,000 years later. Is it really worth maintaining our worship, prayer, and disciplined way of life when the heavenly rewards we are promised seem so delayed?

Peter urges his readers to take a heavenly perspective on time. They had only been waiting 30 years, which, if a day is a thousand years, equates to less than an hour. As for us today, by the same maths we have only been waiting 48 hours! The delay in God's eyes is no longer than the time between the crucifixion and resurrection. That was well worth waiting for!

Patience depends on faith. When we begin to doubt, let us reaffirm our trust in the God who always keeps promises.

Dear God, keep me at peace in poverty of waiting. Amen.

RICHARD MARTIN

You only win when you're singing

You already know these things, dear friends. So be on guard; then you will not be carried away by the errors of these wicked people and lose your own secure footing. Rather, you must grow in the grace and knowledge of our Lord and Saviour Jesus Christ. All glory to him, both now and forever! Amen.

When a team is ahead in a game their supporters chant and celebrate. If they start losing some of the same fans may go quiet. Hence the opposing fans' taunt: 'You only sing when you're winning.' Supporters who want to encourage the players will not warrant that: they sing even more when their team is losing because they believe things can turn round.

Praise is our faith-filled expression of belief in God's unconquerable love even when our individual or corporate lives are tough. The tougher they are the more we praise. That is why the psalmist calls it a sacrifice. Praise is not about volume or fervour. The quiet reaffirmation of our belief in God's goodness is as valid as the music of the most exuberant worship band or thundering cathedral organ.

Praise allows us to experience all the ups and downs of life yet not to be defined by them. To remember who God is and to join in with the worship of heaven, however inadequately, is the way to Christian victory. This is not triumphalism but a quiet confidence that God is eternally kind.

Why does God needs our worship. Is God on a narcissistic ego-trip? Not so: worship is good for us. As we praise, we lift our hearts to God and he fills them with his grace. As the Westminster Shorter Catechism says: 'Man's chief end is to glorify God and to enjoy him forever.'

The football coach will alert his players to the fickle nature of their fans' adulation. It follows, rather than drives, success. Their motivation when times are hard must come from elsewhere. Christian praise relies not on events but on our trust in the eternal nature of God. It is there that we can overcome.

Our wise coach Peter ends his letters on this joyful and defiant note: we only win when we are singing.

Dear God, may my life, my thoughts and my words bring you glory. Amen.

RICHARD MARTIN

John 13—15

The fourth gospel, attributed to the disciple John, also called 'the beloved disciple', contains deep and soul-searching teaching. In the three chapters that we will look at over these next two weeks, John portrays Jesus' definite purpose and divine nature. Jesus' chosen disciples had witnessed unique and stunning signs and wonders, from the water into wine at the Cana wedding (2:11) to the raising of Lazarus (11:43–44). They had watched their master's healing miracles and joined palm-frond-waving crowds as Jesus rode into Jerusalem.

Yes, the miracles Jesus performed created awe and wonder among the people, but in contrast, suspicion, fear, and hostility festered among the temple leaders. As early as chapter 7 we read how the Jewish leaders in Judea 'were looking for a way to kill him' (7:1, NIV). The chief priests and members of the Sanhedrin decided that only by eliminating Jesus could they maintain their own power and position under the Roman occupation.

John 13 begins: 'It was just before the Passover Festival.' What a scene-setter! Thousands of people would have been drawn to Jerusalem for this, the greatest of all Jewish festivals, celebrating God's deliverance of the Hebrew slaves from Egypt. The cosmopolitan crowds drawn to Jerusalem would become agents of God's overall plan and perfect timing. For it was initially through those crowds returning home that news of Jesus, his crucifixion, death, and resurrection spread out around the Mediterranean.

Years after these events, John clearly understood the closing days of Jesus' earthly life to be a parallel with the Passover, when a spotless lamb was sacrificed to atone for the people's sins. Jesus, 'the Lamb of God' (1:36), was sacrificed for the sins of the world.

I have found it helpful to briefly look at four disciples: Peter, Thomas, Philip, and Judas. Their names may be familiar, but we know hardly anything about them. I believe we have much to learn about ourselves from the few verses in which they are mentioned, although, of course, we read about all these people and events through 21st-century eyes.

Come with me, as in mystery and miracle, the Holy Spirit enables us to encounter Jesus afresh, the Messiah proclaimed by the gospel author, John.

ELIZABETH RUNDLE

Pentecost

'If you love me, keep my commands. And I will ask the Father, and he will give you another advocate to help you and be with you forever – the Spirit of truth. The world cannot accept him, because it neither sees him nor knows him. But you know him, for he lives with you and will be in you.'

In biblical times, the annual feast of Pentecost was a joyful highlight, a time of thanksgiving for the wheat harvest. A good harvest secured food, and therefore survival, until the next harvest. Pentecost had also become a thanksgiving for the law given to Moses by God on Mount Sinai. Roll these celebrations together and we see how, in the people's calendar, it was a huge red-letter day.

For our time, Pentecost commemorates the unique fusion between past and present. The prophet Joel, centuries before the coming of Christ, preached his vision of the day of the Lord: 'I will pour out my Spirit on all people' (Joel 2:28). Before his death, Jesus promised his disciples they would receive the gift of the Spirit of truth, a guide, support, and comforter. The apostle Luke records how, 50 days after the resurrection of our Lord, the Holy Spirit entered the group of around 120 believers, huddled together in an upper room in Jerusalem (Acts 2:1–4; see also 1:15). This, together with the promise Jesus had given to his disciples and the fulfilment of Jesus' promise of the Holy Spirit to his followers, ensures the day of Pentecost stands for all time as a red-letter day.

It is often said that God moves in mysterious ways. Let us celebrate today the miracle of God moving in our world and in our lives. In the Old Testament, God's Spirit empowered individuals for particular assignments, and from the day of Pentecost in Acts 2, this empowerment is for every believer in Jesus Christ. As a minister I could not have faced each day and the many difficult situations without the Holy Spirit's strength and guidance.

If you need that strength today, pray these words from an old hymn:
'Be with me when no other friend the mystery of my heart can share;
be always known, when fears descend, by your best name of Comforter'
(A.H. Vine, 1845–1917).

ELIZABETH RUNDLE

The menial task

It was just before the Passover Festival. Jesus knew that the hour had come for him to leave this world and go to the Father... The evening meal was in progress... Jesus... got up from the meal, took off his outer clothing, and wrapped a towel round his waist. After that, he poured water into a basin and began to wash his disciples' feet, drying them with the towel that was wrapped round him.

Quite naturally by evening the disciples' minds were on food. They neglected the niceties of custom in pursuit of supper. These were hungry men. Then – aargh! How embarrassing! Their master, their teacher, their rabbi undertook the servant's task which any one of them should have done for him.

Imagine for a moment the steep pathways, rough tracks, and roads of 2,000 years ago. Leather sandals for those who could afford them, but many would have gone barefoot. How refreshing to have your feet washed. It was the expected courtesy of that time and region. Was it that these men from Galilee were not used to servants or had the excitement of being in the city for Passover and hunger eclipsed any other thoughts? John specifically records 'during supper'. Jesus had given them ample time to act. Then he used this menial task as a supreme teaching aid. It is a teaching that holds meaning in every time and every culture; teaching everyone understands: humility, love, and service. These remain the hallmarks of all who follow Jesus. They are also the hallmarks of compassionate human coexistence regardless of beliefs.

Years ago it was my privilege to walk with a chaplain through a psychogeriatric hospital ward. I shall never forget the chaplain's tenderness as he held a frail hand, held a cup of tea, and wiped a dribbled chin. Let us give thanks today for all the love and service people deliver in our community, the daily tasks of caring no matter what age or need. And let us be inspired by all the goodness in our world. When writing to the first Christians in Ephesus, the apostle Paul wrote begging them to 'be completely humble and gentle; be patient, bearing with one another in love' (Ephesians 4:2).

Lord Jesus, help me lead such a life as this. Amen.

ELIZABETH RUNDLE

Peter's problem

He came to Simon Peter, who said to him, 'Lord, are you going to wash my feet?' Jesus answered, 'You do not know now what I am doing, but later you will understand.' Peter said to him, 'You will never wash my feet.' Jesus answered, 'Unless I wash you, you have no share with me.' Simon Peter said to him, 'Lord, not my feet only but also my hands and my head!'... [Jesus said,] 'For I have set you an example, that you also should do as I have done to you.'

The familiarity of this story causes little disturbance in our hearts when these verses are read in church or at home. We have lost the initial impact, the shock and astonishment of the disciples and early hearers. Previous generations would have totally understood Peter's horror. It was unthinkable that his Lord should touch his feet. Yet John's account has fascinated and challenged over the centuries. The great 16th-century painter Tintoretto was so inspired by this cameo that he painted the subject at least six times.

What was Peter's problem? As men together, they had all trudged the same route into Jerusalem, so naturally their feet were grubby. It seems Peter could not bear the thought of the man he loved and revered seeing that dirt. Embarrassed? Yes. Too proud to admit his need of a wash? Yes. Ashamed that none of them had given Jesus that tender courtesy? Of course: all this and more.

For me, the wonderful truth we take from these verses is that Jesus understood. In so few words we catch a glimpse not only of Jesus' loving patience, but also his complete humility. Only later would the disciples understand that foot-washing was a symbol of spiritual cleansing, a kind of baptism into readiness for the rigours of spreading their Lord's way of life when he was no longer physically with them. It was a powerful example of the humility Jesus expected each of them to show.

Imagine the scene in your mind's eye: eleven other men probably feeling just as uncomfortable as Peter. One of them, Judas, would find Jesus, his Lord, kneeling in front of him, washing his feet. Did Judas meet Jesus' eyes?

Think today of millions of situations where tender washing is necessary.

Thank you, Lord, for gentle, humble hands caring for others. Amen.

ELIZABETH RUNDLE

Perils of temptation

After he received the piece of bread, Satan entered into him. Jesus said to him, 'Do quickly what you are going to do'... Some thought that, because Judas had the common purse, Jesus was telling him, 'Buy what we need for the festival,' or that he should give something to the poor. So, after receiving the piece of bread, he immediately went out. And it was night.

Put aside for a moment your image of Judas' kiss of betrayal in the Garden of Gethsemane. Rather focus with me on the man, Judas Iscariot. What do we know? His father was called Simon and Judas was not from Galilee. Jesus had chosen him and given him responsibility for their 'common purse'. In other words, he was the group's trusted treasurer, a position for a competent and educated man. Judas belonged to that inner band of twelve, travelling with Jesus, listening to his teaching, and witnessing the miracles. Day in, day out, Judas was there.

The gospel author states, 'Satan entered into him' (v. 27). When we read of some dreadful act, we may say of the perpetrator, 'Whatever possessed them?' In the same way, these verses make it plain that evil had possessed the treasurer disciple. Had greed or disillusionment or even ambition gripped Judas? We can never know his motive, but look at this chilling sentence: 'And it was night' (v. 30). John's gospel is full of contrasts, good and evil, rich and poor, light and dark. Those stark words describe Judas leaving Jesus, the light of the world, choosing instead to embrace the darkness of betrayal.

I vividly remember a reflective slide presentation shown in a service. As each photo came up, we said aloud, 'God loves you.' It was easy looking at babies and toddlers, fun looking at smiling sportspeople, touching when kind, elderly faces appeared. Suddenly the screen filled with the picture of a convicted killer. Words we had so readily repeated dried up. It made us think. Judas has been vilified through 2,000 years, but we must not forget our Lord chose him. Our Lord loved him.

Life is full of temptations. Reflect today on choices you have made, temptations you have or have not resisted, and how those choices have impacted on your life.

ELIZABETH RUNDLE

The eleventh commandment?

'Little children, I am with you only a little longer. You will look for me, and as I said to the Jews so now I say to you, "Where I am going, you cannot come." I give you a new commandment, that you love one another. Just as I have loved you, you also should love one another. By this everyone will know that you are my disciples, if you have love for one another.'

In his book *Strength to Love*, Martin Luther King Jr wrote: 'Our responsibility as Christians is to discover the meaning of the command and seek passionately to live it out in our daily lives.' The world has moved on since then. Our world would be inconceivable to the people who gathered around Jesus, yet the challenge and the truth remains unchanged. A closer look at Jesus' words can feel quite unnerving. Our multiuse of the word 'love' covers anything from love of a partner to love of mashed potato. However, the Greek word used in this verse is '*agape*', which denotes a selfless seeking of another's well-being – not our own emotional desire, but a reflection of God's love. It is a love that is willing to be self-sacrificing and unending. This is not some airy-fairy 'wouldn't it be nice' kind of idea, but a command, one every bit as important as the ten brought down from Mount Sinai by Moses.

If that sounds overdramatic, think about the alternative. The first quarter of this century has proved the alternative, with the consequences of hatred brutally thrust into our homes via multiple media. Contrasting themes in John's gospel of good and evil, light and dark, love and hate are not confined to those who call themselves Christian. These are the universal themes of all humanity. And despite barriers of language and lifestyle, everyone understands empathy, gentleness, and compassion. We all know and respect the altruistic devotion groups of people give to their chosen charities. This is where we come close to our Lord's meaning – thinking beyond ourselves to the benefit of others, often total strangers.

We bear responsibility to live out *agape* love, to demonstrate the way to live in peace and harmony. The world is watching.

'Beloved, let us love one another, because love is from God' (1 John 4:7a).

ELIZABETH RUNDLE

Declaration of loyalty

Simon Peter said to him, 'Lord, where are you going?' Jesus answered, 'Where I am going, you cannot follow me now, but you will follow afterwards.' Peter said to him, 'Lord, why can I not follow you now? I will lay down my life for you.' Jesus answered, 'Will you lay down your life for me? Very truly, I tell you, before the cock crows, you will have denied me three times.'

When visiting such an iconic city as Jerusalem, first impressions last a lifetime. Our group arrived in the dark, around midnight, and the excitement made sleep impossible. Before dawn, as I lay in bed, I could hear donkeys braying above the traffic's hum, and then a cock crowed. This Bible story leapt into my mind. Here in Jerusalem, I heard the same sound familiar to Jesus and Peter. We tend to concentrate on Jesus' prediction rather than on Peter's reaction, but I cannot help but think how devastated Peter must have felt by Jesus' words. At that moment in time, Peter was adamant in his loyalty. This was the Peter Jesus had called 'rock' (Matthew 16:18). Impatient, forthright Peter – surely, he would be the last disciple to deny his Lord. Yet in that laser-like phrase Jesus showed his knowledge of human nature.

We want to appear strong, but Jesus knows our weaknesses. Has there been an occasion when circumstances have made us say or do things we never intended? We might make the excuse that it was out of character. Whatever we say or do, the miracle is that Jesus accepts, forgives, and loves us. Peter learnt that truth, but only after plummeting to the depths of despair.

In my early 20s I was told that you never learn anything by success. I resented this gloomy, demoralising statement. However, the older I become, the more I understand the truth of those words.

Ancient psalmists knew the depths of despair, and poets capture the longing to be strong against the world's temptations. For the confirmation of his children, John Ernest Bode (1816–74) wrote a well-loved hymn of encouragement, giving us a prayer for today: 'O Jesus, I have promised to serve you to the end; O give me grace to follow my master and my friend.'

ELIZABETH RUNDLE

Finding the way

'Do not let your hearts be troubled. Believe in God; believe also in me. In my Father's house there are many dwelling places… And if I go and prepare a place for you, I will come again and will take you to myself, so that where I am, there you may be also. And you know the way to the place where I am going.' Thomas said to him, 'Lord, we do not know where you are going…' Jesus said to him, 'I am the way and the truth and the life.'

Among all the disciples, I have a bit of a soft spot for Thomas. Honest, blunt, with a tendency for his glass of life to be half empty, he was nevertheless a loyal disciple. When it became obvious how dangerous it was for Jesus to go back to the city of Jerusalem, it was Thomas who spoke out in his support. He was willing to die with his master (see John 11:16).

I picture Thomas sitting at the back of the group of disciples, muttering in a world-weary voice. He listened intently to Jesus, but Jesus had left out the vital detail – where exactly was he going? Thomas wanted to know, and he wanted to know how to get there. John is definite: it was Thomas who asked the question which must have been in all their minds. This is a follow-up to yesterday, when Peter questioned Jesus. Instead of the answer Peter expected, Jesus made the prediction of Peter's denial. Instead of the answer Thomas expected, Jesus came out with one of the famous 'I am' statements.

This statement was better understood by the disciples and people of that time than it is by us today. The 'way' was used by Moses, Isaiah, and the psalmist to denote God's way, the right and perfect way. 'Truth' is defined in Psalm 119:142, 151, 160 as God's word. And the third great word, 'life', is the very essence of creation. This is one of the most emphatic disclosures of Jesus' unity with God. We can read or say the line so quickly whereas each word carries an awesome meaning. Jesus prepares a place for each of us.

Lord Jesus, there are so many paths, so many distractions.
Help me follow the way, the truth, and the life. Amen.

ELIZABETH RUNDLE

Needing proof

'If you know me, you will know my Father also. From now on you do know him and have seen him'. Philip said to him, 'Lord, show us the Father, and we will be satisfied.' Jesus said to him, 'Have I been with you all this time, Philip, and you still do not know me? Whoever has seen me has seen the Father. How can you say, 'Show us the Father'? Do you not believe that I am in the Father and the Father is in me?'

In church the other Sunday the audiovisual operator was called David, the organist was another David, and the senior steward was also called David. Seldom does a teacher find they have a whole class without duplicating first names. So we should not be surprised the same thing happened in gospel times. Two Philips are mentioned in the New Testament, but the Philip mentioned today was one of the first disciples to be called. His name may not be the first you think of among the disciples, but in John's gospel he is named in several episodes prior to this passage (see 1:43–51; 6:1–15; 12:20–26).

He came from the fishing village of Bethsaida along with the brothers Andrew and Simon Peter, yet Philip was a Greek name. Was that why 'some Greeks' (12:20) approached Philip with their request to see Jesus? Right at the beginning, it was Philip who told Nathanael they had found 'the one' about whom the prophets wrote. Also pragmatic, he warned Jesus there were too many people to feed before he witnessed Jesus feeding the 5,000. Philip, so close to Jesus, witnessed miracles but still needed proof. He would understand a lot better if only he could see the Father. Would not we all?

In those far off times in Jewish history, no one had seen God. In parallel thinking with the Greeks, 'God' was invisible. Philip had not grasped his master's divine mission, even though in these chunks of teaching, Jesus explicitly stated his divinity. Do we sense hurt in Jesus' reply? Before the crucifixion and subsequent resurrection appearances, none of the disciples clearly understood this teaching. It remains an enigma for us, too.

What is your image of God? How do you see God reflected in John's gospel? What question would you ask Jesus?

ELIZABETH RUNDLE

The gift of peace

'All this I have spoken while still with you. But the Advocate, the Holy Spirit, whom the Father will send in my name, will teach you all things and will remind you of everything I have said to you. Peace I leave with you; my peace I give you. I do not give to you as the world gives. Do not let your hearts be troubled and do not be afraid.'

Cartoonists have a genius for creating an arresting picture needing no words of explanation. Sometimes parody, pathos, and satire combine in pictures which stay long in the memory. One such dramatic picture I recently came across depicted scores of Kalashnikov rifles covering the space, pointing in all directions. Only on looking closely did I notice a tiny white, blood-splattered dove, struggling to peek out from behind the wall of lethal weapons. It was a striking indictment on the many wars in our world.

This is the second time in this chapter that Jesus promises his disciples the Holy Spirit. The Holy Spirit would be their guide and help them to remember and understand the gospel message. The Messiah's teaching to turn the world's power-seeking and profiteering into compassion and service. As disciples of today we need the Holy Spirit to teach and direct our lives. We do not understand everything, but by prayer and meditation, the Holy Spirit illuminates the teaching of Jesus to each and every one of us.

The peace Jesus gave was God's peace, which passes all our human understanding. Not just the absence of warfare, but a restorative sense of well-being and wholeness. Everyone wants peace, but not always the numinous peace offered by Jesus Christ.

Time and again, that golden thread of encouragement, the words 'Do not be afraid', pop up in scripture. Jesus was preparing his disciples to be on their own. He would not be physically with them, but they would have an indwelling Counsellor, his Holy Spirit, to conquer their natural apprehension and fear. At the beginning of John 14, Jesus gives a reason for us to have courage: 'Believe in God; believe also in me' (v. 1, NRSV).

'Simply trusting every day… Even when my faith is small, trusting Jesus, that is all' (Edgar Page Stites, 1836–1921).

ELIZABETH RUNDLE

Parting

'You heard me say, "I am going away and I am coming back to you." If you loved me, you would be glad that I am going to the Father, for the Father is greater than I. I have told you now before it happens, so that when it does happen you will believe. I will not say much more to you, for the prince of this world is coming. He has no hold over me.'

Jesus would soon leave his disciples. To be fair to those disciples, they saw no earthly reason why their master should leave them. They could not come to terms with parting and, in the same way, we also find all manner of partings difficult; particularly the parting of death. From our standpoint, with hindsight, we can agree there was no earthly reason for Jesus to die. Here we meet the difference between the earthly and the heavenly. The earthly we might understand. The heavenly can only be viewed through the eyes of faith.

The disciples loved Jesus, so I doubt that any of them were 'glad' he was 'going away'. Parting with those we love is never easy, be it for weeks, years, or losing a loved one beyond our sight to the realm of the life to come. The disciples would have been totally confused by the thought of a coming 'prince' or ruler of the world. Jesus was their lord and master, their ultimate ruler. Who was this prince? And if he would have no hold on Jesus, who would he rule? These are understandable questions many ask today.

Reading these remembered and treasured words of Jesus, do you ever feel he is speaking to you? Do you hear a warning in his words, 'The prince of this world'? Evil influences, which have always been so powerful, have no power over Jesus, and with the help of the Holy Spirit, followers of Jesus will be able to resist that power. The disciples were too full of their own worries to understand what Jesus was saying. Only after Jesus' death and resurrection in the power of the Holy Spirit did they recall and understand those momentous words.

Help me, Lord, to know that evil has no power over me. Amen.

ELIZABETH RUNDLE

The real deal

'I am the true vine, and my Father is the vinegrower. He removes every branch in me that bears no fruit. Every branch that bears fruit he prunes to make it bear more fruit. You have already been cleansed by the word that I have spoken to you. Abide in me as I abide in you. Just as the branch cannot bear fruit by itself unless it abides in the vine, neither can you unless you abide in me.'

Tours of vineyards and talks on viniculture with wine tasting are very popular. The UK alone cultivates 90 varieties of grape. Jesus' use of this simple allegory of the vine followed prophets like Isaiah and Jeremiah. All his listeners understood about vines. Vines were so ingrained in their history that a couple of hundred years before Jesus, the vine emblem was engraved on their Maccabean coins. How wonderful that this horticultural image has never been out of date, ensuring Jesus' teaching is understandable and relevant in our own lives.

However, our approach to the allegory is slightly different from that of the disciples. In their history the people had been likened to vines. Psalm 80:8, for example, says, 'You brought a vine out of Egypt', referring to Moses leading the slaves towards the promised land. But that 'vine' of Israel had not been perfect. The people chose their own way and 'yielded rotten grapes' (Isaiah 5:2). They ignored God's word.

This is the last of Jesus' 'I am' sayings. He took the very symbols scripture accorded to God: light; shepherd; bread; door; resurrection and the life; the way, the truth, and the life; and finally, the vine. Jesus said he was the 'true' vine – not a false prophet but, what we might say today, the genuine article, the real deal. He was the promised Messiah. Familiarity can dull our appreciation of this amazing statement. It is easy to overlook the obvious statement about branches unable to bear fruit on their own. This applies to everyone. It applies to us. Without Jesus Christ we cannot fulfil our God-given potential for bearing the fruits of the Spirit: love, joy, peace, patience, kindness, generosity, faithfulness, gentleness, and self-control.

Think for a while – to what are you attached?
What difference does it make?

ELIZABETH RUNDLE

Staying connected

'I am the vine; you are the branches. Those who abide in me and I in them bear much fruit, because apart from me you can do nothing. Whoever does not abide in me is thrown away like a branch and withers; such branches are gathered, thrown into the fire, and burned... As the Father has loved me, so I have loved you; abide in my love.'

Today's passage contains the lovely old word 'abide'. The likely Aramaic word Jesus would have used is *qewa*, giving the sense of staying around, remaining to the end. The J.B. Phillips translation puts it like this: 'You must go on growing in me and I will grow in you.' There is no tree on earth where branches grow separately from the trunk, yet it is quite a spiritual effort to think of ourselves as branches attached and growing from Jesus himself.

The vivid analogy our Lord gave to his followers sprang from their natural surroundings, with the prevalence of vines, pomegranates, almonds, and olives, and the husbandry necessary for good and healthy crops. In our time, we place the emphasis on a growing, evolving, and maturing relationship with our Lord. We give the greatest thought and time to those who are closest to us. The whole purpose of our growing 'in' Jesus is to offer the 'fruits' of peace and compassion to others.

I often wonder how many times Jesus repeated the words recorded in John's gospel. There were no handy recordings and no pamphlets in first-century Palestine. To register his message deep in the hearts and minds of his hearers, Jesus, the peripatetic teacher and healer, would have repeated his teaching on hillsides, in houses around Galilee, and all the way to Jerusalem. Repetition stressed the importance of his mission and by calling his disciples 'branches', Jesus described the tender and intimate link to himself. We speak of 'branches' of a family tree but often we may feel no direct attachment. With Jesus that is different; the gospel is summed up in this simple analogy of the vine and the branches.

Lord Jesus, I pray for that qewa, *the staying power to grow and remain strong in prayer, faith, and love. Amen.*

ELIZABETH RUNDLE

A central theme

'My command is this: love each other as I have loved you… You are my friends if you do what I command. I no longer call you servants, because a servant does not know his master's business. Instead, I have called you friends… You did not choose me, but I chose you and appointed you so that you might go and bear fruit – fruit that will last… This is my command: love each other.'

Rooted in this command from Jesus, the central theme of love can be traced throughout his ministry of teaching and healing. It is a theme which continues in the Spirit-inspired letters to the early groups of believers. Love – in its widest sense of selfless compassion, concern for the weak and those disregarded by society, and the desire to treat each life with gentle dignity – has to be the bedrock of human interaction. Jesus commanded his followers to love in the way he had loved, a love which embodied acceptance and forgiveness. That can be so hard.

Then Jesus makes the leap from lord and master to call his disciples friends. All those months with them, illustrating his divinity with parables and miracles, demonstrating his God-given power. He hoped they knew 'their master's business'. Jesus had chosen them, the fishermen, the tax collector, and even the one who would betray him – a disparate group indeed. But take a moment to look at our own friends whom we have chosen. Even though they will be so different, they enrich our lives.

Those chosen disciples, his friends, would have their own mission. In the image of this chapter, their mission would be to 'bear fruit': lasting fruit. The seeds they would sow would themselves be perpetuated in the ongoing mission of future disciples, the spreading of God's kingdom of justice, peace, and love.

In 1967, the Beatles were asked to provide a song which could be easily understood by everyone for the first live global television link, broadcast by satellite. The record was an instant hit: 'All you need is love.' Via satellite the programme went out to 400 million people in 25 countries.

'O give thanks to the Lord… his steadfast love endures forever' (Psalm 136:1, NRSV).

ELIZABETH RUNDLE

Belonging to Jesus

'If the world hates you, be aware that it hated me before it hated you. If you belonged to the world, the world would love you as its own. Because you do not belong to the world, but I have chosen you out of the world, therefore the world hates you… It was to fulfil the word that is written in their law, 'They hated me without a cause.'

Jesus was quoting from the Psalms, but God's prophets, like Isaiah, Jeremiah, and Ezekiel, were all also hated. At times even Moses was the object of people's anger. It seems nobody is popular when speaking truth to power.

It is estimated that more than 380 million believers in over 50 countries suffer discrimination and persecution for their faith in Jesus – desecrated churches, worshippers attacked, and thousands murdered. Why is such hatred directed to those who follow the Lord, who taught justice, peace, and compassion?

The troubling evidence of this century is that the age of those consumed with hatred gets ever younger. Each year the United Nations receives reports of children indoctrinated by armed groups at the age of eight and nine. It is a desecration of how life in this beautiful, God-given world should be.

It is a world we share. So what did Jesus mean by saying, 'You do not belong to the world?' Consider for a moment human behaviour devoid of principle, the self-gratification that jolts everything out of perspective. Now consider the way of life Jesus taught, a continual battle to maintain the meaning of the Hebrew word *hesed*, loving kindness. We each have the choice as to how we live.

As we come to the end of these two weeks of notes, I leave you with words from a hymn written in 1848 by the American Quaker John Greenleaf Whittier (1807–92): 'Follow with reverent steps the great example, each loving life a psalm of gratitude. Love shall tread out the baleful fire of anger and in its ashes plant the tree of peace.'

ELIZABETH RUNDLE

2 Corinthians 1—7

The epistle we know as Paul's second letter to the Corinthians was in fact probably his fourth. (Yes, it gets complicated!) The first, mentioned in 1 Corinthians 5:9, is a lost letter, and the second is the one we know as 1 Corinthians. This was written from Ephesus in about AD53 to the congregation Paul had founded two years earlier in Corinth (Acts 18), the capital city of the Roman province of Achaia in present-day southern Greece.

Soon after Paul wrote 1 Corinthians, he sent his trusted co-worker Timothy to Corinth, who returned with a troubling report that a group of Jewish Christian missionaries – 'false apostles' (2 Corinthians 11:13, NIV) – had arrived in Corinth and were criticising Paul and questioning his apostolic credentials. At some point, Paul then travelled to Corinth, perhaps immediately so to defend himself against their attack on his name and to uphold his own authority. He later described this as a 'painful visit' (2 Corinthians 2:1), apparently because someone there offended him in some way during his stay. Paul then wrote a third (now lost) letter, a stinging rebuke to his flock, written 'with many tears' (2 Corinthians 2:4).

This third letter was carried to Corinth by Titus, another of Paul's trusted companions, but after Titus had set off with it, Paul began to be sorry he had sent it. His mind would not rest until he knew how it had been received. When Paul finally met up with Titus in Macedonia, Titus had good news: the tearful letter had been completely effective; it was just what had been needed and had its desired effect. The Corinthians had repented and were now solidly behind Paul. Paul was overjoyed by this news and responded by writing a fourth letter, our 2 Corinthians, with an outpouring of open-hearted affection. Written from Macedonia in about AD55, it is the joyful and conciliatory sequel to the tearful letter.

The epistle is full of passion and emotion, from which we can learn much about Paul's weaknesses and vulnerabilities as well as his great love for the Corinthians. Though we have time for only the first half of the letter over the next two weeks, we shall encounter sorrow and joy, reproach and praise, and unquestionably some of Paul's most finely crafted theology.

TIM HEATON

A partnership in the gospel

Paul, an apostle of Christ Jesus by the will of God, and Timothy our brother, To the church of God that is in Corinth, together with all the saints throughout Achaia: Grace to you and peace from God our Father and the Lord Jesus Christ. Blessed be the God and Father of our Lord Jesus Christ, the Father of mercies and the God of all consolation, who consoles us in all our affliction, so that we may be able to console those who are in any affliction with the consolation with which we ourselves are consoled by God.

The co-sender of this letter is Timothy, a convert of Paul's first missionary journey who became one of his closest co-workers. He was present with Paul when the church in Corinth was established and later returned there as Paul's emissary and an active leader in the church. It is likely that Timothy was regularly with Paul while this letter was being written, and because of Paul's great confidence in him, he might even have played a part in its composition.

The letter is addressed to the church in Corinth, along with 'the saints throughout Achaia' (v. 1). Achaia was the Roman province of which Corinth was the capital, and 'saints' was a popular early label for Christians, literally 'holy ones'. Saints on earth were sanctified and set apart in the service of God and God's people. The church in Corinth would not have been a church as we know it, but would have comprised several groups of believers who met in the homes of various members, such as that of Aquila and Prisca, who are mentioned in 1 Corinthians 16:19.

Through all the dangers and difficulties endured for the sake of the gospel, Timothy sought to mirror the selfless leadership of Paul. Their relationship became a devoted partnership in the gospel. It fostered an unselfish commonality of purpose, in which they were sustained above all things by the comfort and consolation of God – something for which Paul never neglects to be thankful for.

Do you have a close colleague or co-worker, either in your church life or a secular sphere, who helps bring the true satisfaction that comes from getting the job done? If so, give thanks to God for them now.

TIM HEATON

Be true to your word

Since I was sure of this, I wanted to come to you first, so that you might have a double favour; I wanted to visit you on my way to Macedonia and to come back to you from Macedonia and have you send me on to Judea. Was I vacillating when I wanted to do this? Do I make my plans according to ordinary human standards, ready to say 'Yes, yes' and 'No, no' at the same time? As surely as God is faithful, our word to you is not 'Yes and No'.

We get a sense here of the tense situation that had arisen between Paul and the Corinthians. Paul had planned to make a third visit to Corinth but changed his mind. As a result, the Corinthians have accused him not only of 'vacillating' – saying 'Yes' one day and 'No' the next – but also of making plans 'according to ordinary human standards' (v. 17). The charge is that Paul, an apostle of Christ, does not keep his promises as Christ keeps his. Moreover, if he is not true to his word about his travel plans, is anything that he has told them about the Son of God actually true?

For them to confront their apostle in this manner is a measure of the gulf that had opened between them. If my bishop had to go back on an agreement to visit my church, I certainly would not chastise her and suggest that nothing matters to her but the whim of the moment! I would accept that if the bishop was forced to change her plans, she would have good reason for doing so.

Paul assures them that he is faithful as God is faithful. In all his dealings with the Corinthian church, from preaching the gospel to discussing his travel plans, his word has been true. Far from adopting worldly standards he has structured his whole life, in things both great and small, to his responsibilities as an apostle of Christ. He claims to be not guilty of vacillation, but he must still explain why he changed his mind about visiting them. We shall find out his reason tomorrow.

There is no 'Yes' and 'No' with God.
All the promises of God find their 'Yes' in Jesus.

TIM HEATON

Tough love

So I made up my mind not to make another visit that causes you grief. For if I cause you grief, who is there to make me glad but the one whom I have grieved? And I wrote as I did, so that when I came, I might not suffer grief from those who should have made me rejoice, for I am confident about all of you, that my joy would be the joy of all of you. For I wrote to you out of much distress and anguish of heart and with many tears, not to cause you grief but to let you know the abundant love that I have for you.

In order to spare them another painful visit, Paul decided not to call in on the Corinthians on his way to Macedonia. We know nothing for certain about this painful visit, but we could speculate that Paul went as soon as he received the troubling report from Timothy about the false apostles who had arrived in Corinth and were criticising Paul and his teaching.

It is also plausible that Paul went to demand obedience from a church member who was living incestuously (1 Corinthians 5:1) but was slighted by this person. Whatever the reasons for the visit, it seems to have been a complete failure: someone took the lead in defying his authority, possibly but not necessarily the incestuous man – the identity of this person and the details of his actions are unknown – leaving Paul deeply humiliated, and the Corinthians remained more attracted to other teachers than to Paul.

Further action was needed, so Paul attempted to achieve by letter what he had been unable to achieve in the flesh. He sent a stinging rebuke to his flock, his third (now lost) letter, written 'with many tears' (v. 4). This was tough love, addressing their defiant behaviour but intended to help them in the long run. Paul was at risk of losing all that he had worked so hard for. The tearful letter was a last-ditch attempt to restore his relationship – and it worked!

Love perseveres (1 Corinthians 13:7), it never gives up. Tough love may be necessary when it is the only way left to hold on to those we love the most.

TIM HEATON

Forgiveness for the offender

But if anyone has caused grief, he has caused it not to me but to some extent – not to exaggerate it – to all of you. This punishment by the majority is enough for such a person; so now instead you should forgive and console him, so that he may not be overwhelmed by even worse grief. So I urge you to reaffirm your love for him. I wrote for this reason: to test you and to know whether you are obedient in everything. Anyone whom you forgive, I also forgive. In fact, what I have forgiven, if I have forgiven anything, has been for your sake in the presence of Christ.

While the tearful letter achieved the restoration of good relations with the Corinthian church as a whole, a major goal of 2 Corinthians is Paul's reconciliation with the individual whose behaviour on his last visit caused him – and to some extent the whole church – so much pain.

The tearful letter had been so severe and had stung the Corinthians so sharply that they had gone too far in the opposite direction. Having previously turned a blind eye to improper behaviour in the church and shown such indifference to Paul's authority, they have now gone overboard in trying to vindicate themselves by making a scapegoat of the offender. Paul says the man has now been punished enough and urges them to forgive and console him. He says that his demand that the wrongdoer be disciplined was not out of any personal resentment against him but to test whether the church would be obedient to their apostle Paul.

The New Testament proclaims tirelessly the importance of forgiveness. Forgiveness is a redemptive rather than a destructive action; retribution is a negative and damaging response, whereas forgiveness releases and delivers the offender from any guilt for the offence. It is wholly positive and restorative. Forgiveness is what God in Christ has shown us, and we in turn must forgive others if we are to be reconciled to them and to God. Paul (formerly Saul), the erstwhile persecutor of the church, knew this as well as anyone.

'Bear with one another and, if anyone has a complaint against another, forgive each other; just as the Lord has forgiven you, so you also must forgive' (Colossians 3:13).

TIM HEATON

The fragrance of Christ

But thanks be to God, who in Christ always leads us in triumphal procession and through us spreads in every place the fragrance that comes from knowing him. For we are the aroma of Christ to God among those who are being saved and among those who are perishing: to the one group a fragrance from death to death, to the other a fragrance from life to life. Who is qualified for these things? For we are not peddlars of God's word like so many, but as persons of sincerity, as persons sent from God, we are speaking in Christ before God.

The triumphal procession evokes an image of a victorious Roman general parading the vanquished foe. Paul hints at the success of his own ministry throughout the eastern Mediterranean region, conquering wherever he has preached the gospel. Yet it is not him but God in Christ who leads the procession: it is the gospel that conquers, not the apostle. As Paul so often reminds us, the credit is God's – thanks be to God and to God be the glory!

The 'fragrance' (v. 14) is the knowledge of God spread by the preaching of the gospel. This alludes to the use of incense in Roman victory parades – pleasing to the spectators but to the captives a harbinger of their imminent death. In the same way, the fragrance is different to those who are being saved by the gospel and those who are perishing (that is, unbelievers): to the former it is the aroma of life and to the latter the stench of death.

'We are the aroma', writes Paul (v. 15) – not him and his co-workers in their own right but as those who spread the fragrance of Christ. So Paul asks: 'Who is qualified for these things?' (v. 16). In other words, who is competent to preach such a gospel? The answer, of course, is Paul and not the false apostles. They are merely 'peddlars of God's word' (v. 17). They are imposters and charlatans, phonies and frauds. They have not been sent by God as has the apostle. The Corinthians must take their lead from him.

There is only one gospel, the gospel of Christ crucified, and its message calls for a decision that has life-or-death consequences.

TIM HEATON

Ministers of the new covenant

Now if the ministry of death, chiselled in letters on stone tablets, came in glory so that the people of Israel could not gaze at Moses' face because of the glory of his face, a glory now set aside, how much more will the ministry of the Spirit come in glory? For if there was glory in the ministry of condemnation, much more does the ministry of justification abound in glory! Indeed, what once had glory has in this respect lost its glory because of the greater glory, for if what was set aside came through glory, much more has the permanent come in glory!

When Moses came down from Mount Sinai with the two stone tablets bearing the ten commandments, his face shone because he had been in the presence of God, and he put a veil on his face. This might have been to prevent the Israelites from seeing that the brightness faded over time and was recharged each time Moses went into the tent of meeting to speak with God (Exodus 34:29–35).

Paul is comparing the splendour of the new covenant in Christ with the fading glory of the old covenant under Moses, the word 'glory' bearing all the connotations of radiance, light, and brilliance. The glory of the old covenant, like the gleaming of Moses' face, had faded over time and now its glory – splendid as it was – has given way to the greater and unfading glory of the new. The old has been outshone by the surpassing splendour of the gospel, which is permanent and can never be eclipsed.

The old covenant he calls the 'ministry of death' and the 'ministry of condemnation'; the new he calls the 'ministry of the Spirit' and the 'ministry of justification'. This points to what Paul regarded as the destructive effects of the law of Moses, because it set one up to fail and convicted the lawbreaker. The gospel, on the other hand, gives us life in the Spirit through justification, which means being put in a right relationship with God through our faith in Jesus Christ.

'I was once alive apart from the law, but when the commandment came, sin revived and I died, and the very commandment that promised life proved to be death to me' (Romans 7:9–10).

TIM HEATON

The gospel light

And even if our gospel is veiled, it is veiled to those who are perishing. In their case the god of this world has blinded the minds of the unbelievers, to keep them from seeing clearly the light of the gospel of the glory of Christ, who is the image of God. For we do not proclaim ourselves; we proclaim Jesus Christ as Lord and ourselves as your slaves for Jesus' sake. For it is the God who said, 'Light will shine out of darkness,' who has shone in our hearts to give the light of the knowledge of the glory of God in the face of Christ.

Moses covered his shining face with a veil each time he finished speaking with the Israelites and removed it whenever he went into the tent of meeting to speak with God. In this way, continuing yesterday's simile, the glory of the old covenant under Moses had become hidden or obscured. Now the light of the glory of God shines not in the veiled face of Moses but in the unveiled face of Jesus.

Why would Paul now suggest that the *gospel* is 'veiled' (v. 3)? Perhaps because he had been accused of grandiloquence (we might agree), or because his message lacked clear expression and was obscured by too much rhetoric. Or perhaps it was because he believed that the sufferings he had endured for the sake of the gospel – 'our gospel' as distinct from that being peddled by the false apostles – had led to its rejection by some. Perhaps it was a bit of both. In any case, the minds of these unbelievers have, in truth, been 'blinded' (veiled) by Satan, 'the god of this world' (v. 4).

The glory of the gospel comes neither from the wisdom nor the well-being of those who proclaim it but from the presence of God's power working through it. 'We do not proclaim ourselves,' says Paul (v. 5); the glory is God's, and the glory of the message does not mean that the messenger should be glorified. The message is powerful; we, the messengers, are not.

'Then God said, "Let there be light," and there was light' (Genesis 1:3). The gospel light is as much the creation of God as the light that God called into existence in the beginning.

TIM HEATON

Treasure in clay jars

But we have this treasure in clay jars, so that it may be made clear that this extraordinary power belongs to God and does not come from us. We are afflicted in every way but not crushed, perplexed but not driven to despair, persecuted but not forsaken, struck down but not destroyed, always carrying around in the body the death of Jesus, so that the life of Jesus may also be made visible in our bodies. For we who are living are always being handed over to death for Jesus's sake, so that the life of Jesus may also be made visible in our mortal flesh.

The treasure – we know from yesterday's reading – is 'the light of the gospel of the glory of Christ' (v. 4), and we are the clay jars within which this treasure is carried. While the container is relatively worthless, the contents are priceless. This continues the contrast between the glory of the message and the inadequacy of the messenger: the gospel treasure has been entrusted to frail mortals. Yet it is precisely because of this – our very weakness – that we know the power of the gospel comes from God and not from us.

God's life-giving power is displayed in Paul's suffering. Although troubles pressed on him from every quarter, he never found himself crushed, despairing, forsaken, or destroyed. He was sustained in his ministry by Christ's resurrection life. Moreover, the message and the messenger are drawn together in a remarkable relationship: Paul's afflictions are an extension of Christ's and his ministry reflects Christ's *because* it is sacrificial and self-giving. He carries in his body the death of Jesus, so that the life of Jesus may also be seen in him.

Sufferings are not only for apostles. Paul's hardships are typical of others', even perhaps your own. It means that your life of ministry and service points people to Christ because it replicates the pattern of Christ's. Christian ministry is cross-shaped. Paul's story is part of a much larger story, the story of all of us who suffer with and for our crucified, risen, and ascended Lord.

It is not a bad thing to be frail and vulnerable, because this allows God to demonstrate his power more effectively through us: 'power is made perfect in weakness' (2 Corinthians 12:9).

TIM HEATON

Momentary affliction and eternal glory

But just as we have the same spirit of faith that is in accordance with scripture – 'I believed, and so I spoke' – we also believe, and therefore we also speak, because we know that the one who raised Jesus will also raise us with Jesus and will present us with you in his presence. Indeed, everything is for your sake, so that grace, when it has extended to more and more people, may increase thanksgiving, to the glory of God. So we do not lose heart. Even though our outer nature is wasting away, our inner nature is being renewed day by day.

Although Paul hopes for a future splendour, he does not enjoy it now: his outer nature is wasting away. Even so, he does not lose heart, because he knows that his present suffering is meaningful for the coming glory. His inner nature is being renewed day by day by the life-giving Spirit who dwells within him. He knows he must go on serving others – 'everything is for your sake' (v. 15) – and in this he mirrors Jesus, who came not to be served but to serve. His own troubles must not prevail.

Not even the prospect of death can diminish Paul's resilience, and the source of his strength is his faith in God, who can raise the dead: 'the one who raised Jesus will also raise us' (v. 14). Paul has dwelled much in this letter on the afflictions and hardships of his ministry, echoing the sufferings of Jesus, but now he redirects our thoughts to the promise of resurrection and new life – also the experience of Jesus. The centre of our faith is a crucifix behind which stands a tomb that is empty.

Paraphrasing Psalm 116:10 ('I kept my faith, even when I said…'), Paul draws on 'the same spirit of faith' (v. 13) when he voices the certainty of resurrection: because God raised Jesus, we know that we too shall be raised. Therefore, do not lose heart, do not give up. Our present suffering is only momentary and is preparing us for an everlasting glory beyond all measure. The visible is temporary, the invisible is eternal.

'Everything will be okay in the end. If it's not okay, it's not the end' (John Lennon, 1940–80).

TIM HEATON

Restoring divine communion

So if anyone is in Christ, there is a new creation: everything old has passed away; look, new things have come into being! All this is from God, who reconciled us to himself through Christ and has given us the ministry of reconciliation; that is, in Christ God was reconciling the world to himself, not counting their trespasses against them, and entrusting the message of reconciliation to us. So we are ambassadors for Christ, since God is making his appeal through us; we entreat you on behalf of Christ, be reconciled to God.

We have seen already how important it was for Paul to be reconciled to the Corinthian church as a whole and to his individual wrongdoer in particular. Now he urges the Corinthians to be reconciled to God. Paul's opponents – the false apostles – have not only succeeded in alienating the Christian community from Paul but also influenced them to such a negative extent that the church is in danger of alienating itself from God.

Authentic Christian ministry bears the hallmark of reconciliation. Just as God took the initiative to reconcile the world to himself through Christ's death on the cross, restoring God's relationship with humanity, so Paul puts reconciliation at the very heart of his ministry. Those who preach reconciliation must also practise it, and this is precisely what Paul is doing in his relationship with the Corinthians. In this he sees himself as an 'ambassador for Christ' (v. 20), doing what God himself does as reconciler.

The new life we have in Christ is so revolutionary it amounts to 'a new creation' (v. 17), a new birth. It demands viewing human life in an altogether different way: no longer is it to be defined by individual happiness and fulfilment but by service to others; no longer by a prideful inclination that leads to alienation from God but by a self-emptying that leads to reconciliation with God. The heartbeat of Paul's ministry is the good news of reconciliation, a ministry based on the pattern of God's reconciling work in Christ.

Reconciliation involves listening to people's opposing attitudes and beliefs, their strongly held convictions and feelings. Can you see how important this is for today's church, so divided over matters of identity, sexuality, and relationships?

TIM HEATON

Dying yet alive

We are putting no obstacle in anyone's way, so that no fault may be found with our ministry, but as servants of God we have commended ourselves in every way: in great endurance, afflictions, hardships, calamities, beatings, imprisonments, riots, labours, sleepless nights, hunger... We are treated as impostors and yet are true, as unknown and yet are well known, as dying and look – we are alive, as punished and yet not killed, as sorrowful yet always rejoicing, as poor yet making many rich, as having nothing and yet possessing everything.

Paul appeals for a positive response from the Corinthians to his and Timothy's ministry: 'We have commended ourselves in every way' (v. 4). This self-praise is evident throughout the letter, quite understandably, because he is writing to defend himself against the accusations of the false apostles and to assert the trustworthiness of his own conduct. His authority and reliability have been called into question, and the Corinthians need reassurances.

Paul insists he has given no one any excuse for rejecting the gospel on account of shortcomings in his proclamation, integrity, or behaviour. The suffering and crucified Christ has always been the model for his ministry, which embodies in the world its contradictory revelation of God's power. Paul lists nine forms of suffering that tell of his great endurance (vv. 4–5). His daily exposure to danger and possible death, sharing in Christ's passion, attest to the genuineness of his apostleship.

Moreover, his lot only appears wretched when viewed by worldly standards. The seven opposing clauses that follow (vv. 8–10) contrast the *outward* appearance – imposters, unknown, dying, punished, sorrowful, poor, and having nothing – with the true and greater *inner* reality of the heart – true, well known, alive, not killed, rejoicing, rich and possessing everything. Appearances can be deceptive. Again we are drawn to Christ on the cross, who appeared to be broken and defeated, but in truth was revealing the power of God. All that is good and true, cherished and treasured, was being put in our reach.

'Those things which are precious are saved only by sacrifice' (David Kenyon Webster, D-Day veteran).

TIM HEATON

The church in the world

Do not be mismatched with unbelievers... What agreement has the temple of God with idols? For we are the temple of the living God, as God said, 'I will live in them and walk among them, and I will be their God, and they shall be my people. Therefore come out from them, and be separate from them, says the Lord, and touch nothing unclean; then I will welcome you, and I will be your father, and you shall be my sons and daughters, says the Lord Almighty.'

The Corinth that Paul evangelised was a port city hosting a large transient population. Like most ancient ports, Corinth possessed a reputation for sexual immorality, and the Christian community struggled to define its identity as the church of God in a complex and sophisticated urban setting. The Corinthians were the first to face the problem that persists for all churches: how to live in faithfulness to God within the freedoms and diverse moral behaviours of a given social world.

Paul appeals to the Corinthians for purity in the life of the church and calls for separation from the world's values: 'Be separate from them, says the Lord' (v. 17). His lengthy excerpt from scripture here is not actually a single passage but a composite quotation drawn from several sources, including Leviticus, Ezekiel, 2 Samuel, and Isaiah. Because God lives and walks among us, we must withdraw from everything that is incompatible with his holiness.

Paul's call is not, however, for a complete retreat from society. The church cannot minister to the world if it is not in the world; rather we must serve the world as we find it. We must continue to associate with those who do not share our kingdom values, but at the same time we must maintain our integrity. As Christians we enjoy the same God-given freewill as everyone else, but our freedom is inevitably limited, especially in how we use our bodies. Our physical life, particularly our sexual activity, must be aligned to our spiritual life, because 'we are the temple of the living God' (v. 16).

'Do you not know that your body is a temple of the Holy Spirit within you, which you have from God, and that you are not your own?' (1 Corinthians 6:19).

TIM HEATON

Joy at the church's repentance

Now I rejoice, not because you were grieved but because your grief led to repentance, for you felt a godly grief, so that you were not harmed in any way by us. For godly grief produces a repentance that leads to salvation and brings no regret, but worldly grief produces death. For see what earnestness this godly grief has produced in you, what eagerness to clear yourselves, what indignation, what alarm, what longing, what zeal, what punishment! At every point you have proved yourselves guiltless in the matter.

Paul's stinging rebuke to his flock – the tearful letter – had been delivered by another of his trusted co-workers, Titus. Written 'out of much distress and anguish of heart' (2 Corinthians 2:4), we might infer that it was penned in some haste, and as soon as Titus had set off with it, Paul began to be sorry that he had sent it. He went through agonies of regret and his 'mind could not rest' (2:13) until he knew how the letter had been received.

When Paul finally met up with Titus in Macedonia, Titus bore good news: the letter had had its desired effect and had been completely successful. The Corinthians had repented and affirmed their love for Paul and their loyalty to him. It seems that tough love worked; the letter had been just what was needed. Reconciliation had been achieved, and the Corinthians were now solidly behind Paul once more.

Paul was overjoyed to hear Titus' news and immediately writes a further letter – this one, 2 Corinthians – in which he responds with an outpouring of delight and affection. The grief that the tearful letter had caused them was only temporary; the pain was but a means to an end. Moreover, it was a 'godly grief' (vv. 9–11), a grief that accords with God's will because it results in repentance and a change of heart leading to salvation. It brings no regret. Though Paul had once been sorry he had sent the tearful letter, he does not regret it now.

Can you think of a similar situation in which you wrote or said something – in haste or anger – bitterly regretting it later, only to find it had a beneficial effect and produced a constructive outcome in the end?

TIM HEATON

Trust vindicated

In this we have found consolation. In addition to our own consolation, we rejoiced still more at the joy of Titus, because his mind has been set at rest by all of you. For if I have been somewhat boastful about you to him, I was not put to shame, but just as everything we said to you was true, so our boasting to Titus has proved true as well. And his heart goes out all the more to you, as he remembers the obedience of all of you and how you welcomed him with fear and trembling. I rejoice because I have complete confidence in you.

Having worried so much and for so long that his relationship with the Corinthians had broken down, Paul's relief is palpable now that he knows he is reconciled to them. It is a measure of the great love and affection that he had for the Corinthian church, a reflection of Christ's love for them. The tearful letter had been sent to test their submission to Paul's authority, and now his praise of their obedience indicates that they passed the test.

His trust and confidence in the Corinthians have been vindicated. He now has such pride in them he has boasted about them to Titus. But such expressions of confidence are not given completely freely; they serve to create a sense of obligation on the part of the Corinthians to remain loyal and obedient to Paul in future, as well as priming them to agree to the requests that are to come in the second half of the letter.

The epistle continues for another six chapters, but we must leave all that for another day. We can end this series of notes by reflecting on what we have learned about Paul, the great apostle, as a person. Notwithstanding his unparalleled ability and power in proclaiming the gospel, we have encountered a man sensitive to criticism and keen to be loved, fearful of rejection and needful of affirmation, someone who can bitterly regret his words and actions and worry endlessly just like everyone else does. In short, we have found a man who is entirely human, just like you and me.

Thank God for Paul. Thank God for Christ's church,
built on the foundation of the apostles.

TIM HEATON

Abraham: Genesis 12—25

We acknowledge Abraham as a great patriarch and father of Judaism, Christianity, and Islam. Yet many people today find the idea of patriarchy difficult, questioning the concept of unchallenged hierarchy as a way of ordering society. Where does this leave us with the great biblical patriarch?

It may be more helpful to think of him not so much as the *head* of three religions, but rather as their *root*. A head suggests someone who controls things from the top down. A root suggests someone who is in a process of growth. As we explore some aspects of Abraham's story over the coming weeks, we will see this growth in action, including its missteps. We will begin to see his life as an evolving and deepening journey of faith, from which we too have much to learn.

Abraham's journey begins when he is called by God to leave his home in Haran and set out on an unpredictable journey to an unknown destination. Perhaps you too have had to leave a familiar situation and risk a move into the unknown, maybe through force of circumstance or following a call you have also recognised as speaking to your soul. We will all experience, many times over, the pain of having to leave our comfort zone and venture into the unknown.

Abraham, his wife Sarah, and his nephew Lot become aliens in search of a place to pitch their tents and graze their flocks. Mistakes are made that hurt and deceive others. Their integrity is compromised, and they face the consequences of their choices. This is all part of the growing process.

Eventually a divine intervention occurs that changes not just their names but the whole direction of their journey. It comes with an unlikely promise. Abraham learns to surrender to God's guiding, even when it seems to him both improbable and unreasonable. Both his sons, God's covenant assures him – the firstborn, Ishmael, born to the slave Hagar, and the second, Isaac, born to Sarah – are to become the progenitors of great nations.

At the close of our brief journey we find these brothers, side by side, as they bury their father. Joined in their grief, subsequently to be divided by history, but forever held in God's heart and God's covenant.

MARGARET SILF

Leaving the comfort zone

Now the Lord said to Abram, 'Go from your country and your kindred and your father's house to the land that I will show you. I will make of you a great nation, and I will bless you and make your name great, so that you will be a blessing. I will bless those who bless you, and the one who curses you I will curse, and in you all the families of the earth shall be blessed.' So Abram went, as the Lord had told him, and Lot went with him. Abram was seventy-five years old when he departed from Haran.

It is hard to imagine how Abram must have felt when faced with this divine command to leave behind everything that was familiar – kinsfolk, friends, and land – and set off into a completely unknown and unpredictable future. Not to mention how his wife Sarai was likely to react to such a move at their considerably advanced age.

Calls to leave our comfort zones come in many different guises. Sometimes there is no choice, as, it appears, there was no choice for Abram and Sarai, given the urgency of God's instruction. Many people, especially older folk, are compelled for a whole variety of reasons to leave their familiar lives behind at an age when adapting to new situations is very difficult. Sometimes the call is gentler, more like an invitation, to venture into a new place or occupation or changing family circumstances.

However it happens, leaving our comfort zone is never easy, and yet it is often precisely when we do so that we discover new possibilities. And so it is for Abram. God promises him a vision beyond anything he could imagine and a journey that will be transformative not only for him but for all his people.

So Abram sets his gaze on the distant horizon and, along with his wife and his nephew Lot, embarks upon this life-changing adventure, surrendering safety and security and embracing challenge and change – exchanging his sunset years for the possibility and promise of a new dawn.

A ship never discovered new lands without leaving safe harbour. When the call comes for us, may we, like Abram, risk boarding the ship rather than staying safely in the port.

MARGARET SILF

Dispossessed aliens

Now there was a famine in the land. So Abram went down to Egypt to reside there as an alien, for the famine was severe in the land. When he was about to enter Egypt, he said to his wife Sarai, 'I know well that you are a woman beautiful in appearance, and when the Egyptians see you, they will say, 'This is his wife'; then they will kill me, but they will let you live. Say you are my sister, so that it may go well with me because of you and that my life may be spared on your account.'

No longer in the safety of his homeland, Abram has become a wandering alien, hoping to settle in Egypt. Resettling in a strange land, however, is no easy matter. As an alien he has no documentation, no name, no rights, no recognised identity – a plight shared by millions of people in today's fractured and often hostile world.

Trouble comes very soon. There is a harsh famine in Egypt. Abram, like today's asylum seekers, knows that he will need to have his wits about him to survive. He has been called to trust God and God's promise, but he is not yet ready for that. Instead he tackles the problem in his own way.

Even allowing for the cultural differences between our world and Abram's, it would be hard to endorse the trick he devises to keep himself safe. If he enters Egypt with a wedded wife, he knows he will be killed and Sarai taken into a harem, but if she says she is his sister, they will just take her and leave him alone.

The brutal truth is that he is saving his own skin by sacrificing his wife's freedom, even though the harem awaits her whether she is his wife or his sister. Even more seriously, he is beginning their journey with a deliberate deception.

When we find ourselves in desperate need or imminent danger, we become much more vulnerable to the temptation to act deviously. Abram makes what is an entirely self-focused choice which compromises not only his wife but his own integrity.

Trusting our own judgement can lead us badly astray.
May we learn to trust the deeper wisdom that comes from God.

MARGARET SILF

Choices have consequences

But the Lord afflicted Pharaoh and his house with great plagues because of Sarai, Abram's wife. So Pharaoh called Abram and said, 'What is this you have done to me? Why did you not tell me that she was your wife? Why did you say, "She is my sister," so that I took her for my wife? Now then, here is your wife, take her, and be gone.' And Pharaoh gave his men orders concerning him, and they set him on the way with his wife and all that he had. So Abram went up from Egypt, he and his wife and all that he had and Lot with him, into the Negeb.

Bad choices have consequences, and deception will eventually be exposed. The trick that Abram has played to ensure his own safety has jeopardised their chances of settling in Egypt. Pharaoh exposes the lie and calls him to account. The result of this confrontation is that they are both banished from Egypt and sent on their way once more, with nephew Lot and whatever they can carry. The future looks bleak. God's promise must have seemed like a distant dream.

As we think of these departing refugees being sent off into the Negev desert, we cannot avoid seeing the present equivalent in our world today. What is love asking of us in our ways of engaging with the desperate migrants in our own times? It happens, inevitably, that some people seeking refuge in our more comfortable countries fall short, like Abram, of our standards of conduct, and they face deportation. Far more frequently, innocent people are driven out into the desert through no fault of their own.

So Abram, Sarai, and Lot face another exile, another leaving behind of what they had hoped would be a safe haven. This time there is no hope of a relatively agreeable resettlement in another country, but only the unforgiving terrain of the Negev desert.

Perhaps Abram is beginning to learn from his experience as a dispossessed alien, but the learning curve has only just begun, and it will be a steep one.

When the consequences of our selfish choices come back to haunt us, may we honestly acknowledge our failures and focus on the onward journey with God as our guide.

MARGARET SILF

Too much to share

Now Lot, who went with Abram, also had flocks and herds and tents, and the land could not support both of them living together because their possessions were so great that they could not live together. Thus strife arose between the herders of Abram's livestock and the herders of Lot's livestock. At that time the Canaanites and the Perizzites lived in the land. Then Abram said to Lot, 'Let there be no strife between you and me and between your herders and my herders, for we are kindred. Is not the whole land before you? Separate yourself from me.'

Abram and Lot did not travel empty-handed, but with their 'flocks and herds and tents'. In fact it seems that what they lacked in security they made up for in livestock. So much so that they soon needed more land for grazing. The old problem, that has been the cause of so much strife in human life, causes strife between Abram and Lot. They have grown out of the available land, and as wanderers there is no way to expand their territory by force.

History has repeatedly shown that excessive possessions frequently lead to conflict. Abram and Lot find themselves in competition for the available resources. Their respective herders are fighting over the grazing rights, and there are other tribes in the area who also expect fair grazing for their herds. The more we have to defend, the more defensive we become. And the more we have, the more we want, which can lead to vicious competition. Sometimes those who have little are the most generous in sharing what little they have. Those with nothing to lose are more ready to learn to live with others in mutual interdependence.

On the global stage, this dynamic can easily escalate into widespread warfare. Abram, however, wants to prevent conflict with a family member. Strife with kinsfolk spreads like a plague to the wider community, and this must be avoided. Abram is learning and growing as he makes the journey into which God has called him. He therefore suggests that he and Lot go their separate ways, to pre-empt any further conflict.

May we honestly examine our own relationship with wealth,
lest we become possessive, and divided from our own best selves.

MARGARET SILF

Sarai's solution

Now Sarai, Abram's wife, bore him no children. She had an Egyptian slave whose name was Hagar, and Sarai said to Abram, 'You see that the Lord has prevented me from bearing children; go in to my slave; it may be that I shall obtain children by her'... He went in to Hagar, and she conceived, and when she saw that she had conceived, she looked with contempt on her mistress. Then Sarai said to Abram, 'May the wrong done to me be on you!'... Then Sarai dealt harshly with [Hagar], and she ran away from her.

Sarai is also part of this story, and part of the destiny into which she and Abram have been called. She too must grow and learn as they travel. In today's reading we learn how she, too, tries to solve her problem in her own way.

Sarai's preoccupation is not with the herds and the grazing rights but with her own infertility. We can imagine her pondering this issue until she comes up with what, to us, sounds like a preposterous suggestion (though we should be wary of making judgements about a culture and a time that are foreign to us). She suggests that Abram use Hagar as a surrogate in order to provide the much-wanted child, upon whose existence God's promise appears to depend.

Abram concurs and Hagar conceives, and then begins to treat her mistress with contempt. The enraged Sarai turns on Abram with her angry reproaches and, in her frustration, behaves unkindly towards Hagar.

Once again we see that bad choices have consequences, and what seemed like a solution turns into an even bigger problem. And not only a problem for Abram, Sarai, and Hagar, but in it we find the seeds of a split between Sarai and Hagar and their sons Isaac and Ishmael, the repercussions of which reverberate down the ages.

Once again we are confronted, along with our wandering couple, with the truth that choices focused on our own advantage or satisfaction will never, ultimately, end well. Will Sarai learn this necessary lesson? Will we?

When we make our choices, may we have the grace to ask:
'Whose kingdom am I serving by this choice – God's, or my own?'

MARGARET SILF

A radical intervention

When Abram was ninety-nine years old, the Lord appeared to Abram and said to him, 'I am God Almighty; walk before me, and be blameless. And I will make my covenant between me and you and will make you exceedingly numerous.' Then Abram fell on his face, and God said to him, 'As for me, this is my covenant with you: You shall be the ancestor of a multitude of nations. No longer shall your name be Abram, but your name shall be Abraham, for I have made you the ancestor of a multitude of nations.'

Time has moved on 24 years since Abram was first called by God to leave his home and travel into an unknown future. We might think of these years as his apprenticeship in trusting in God's guidance in the wilderness of his experience. Today we arrive at a momentous turning point.

This radical change of direction begins with another instruction from God. Abram has obeyed, with some major distractions and aberrations, the command to leave the known and walk on into the unknown. Now the instruction is to be blameless. The promise is for fruitfulness beyond anything he could imagine. He is to be the progenitor of many nations. This promise, we note, is given to a man of very advanced age whose wife is infertile.

However improbable the promise, Abram does not protest, but instead falls to the ground in surrender. This is a point of conversion that will change the direction of travel.

This momentous change is marked by a change of name. From now on, God says, Abram will be known as Abraham. The wayward son has now been named by a loving parent. The man who was a nameless alien is now adopted into a new identity. When children are adopted, their adopting parents often change their names. God's change of Abram's name signifies that he is no longer a dispossessed wanderer but an adopted son of God.

Once this change has taken place, the impossible becomes possible, the improbable becomes inevitable. Abram's story reminds us that it is never too late to change direction.

May we be alert and attentive to the signs that warn us that we are on the wrong path.

MARGARET SILF

Unexpected guests

The Lord appeared to Abraham by the oaks of Mamre, as he sat at the entrance of his tent in the heat of the day. He looked up and saw three men standing near him. When he saw them, he ran from the tent entrance to meet them and bowed down to the ground. He said, 'My lord, if I have found favour with you, do not pass by your servant. Let a little water be brought, and wash your feet, and rest yourselves under the tree. Let me bring a little bread, that you may refresh yourselves, and after that you may pass on.'

Divine intervention in our lives arrives in many different ways and guises. Today's reading records a totally unexpected event by the oaks of Mamre in Hebron in the present Palestinian West Bank, where Abraham and Sarah have pitched their tent.

If genuine trust is to be established with another person, we need to get to know that person deeply. In pursuit of Abraham's total trust, God therefore arranges to 'drop by for coffee' one day and help Abraham to get to know him more fully. God does this in the form of three strangers.

Abraham sees them approaching from the entrance to his tent. In his position we might perhaps have taken a closer look, wondered who this might be, been a bit suspicious, and maybe hesitated or even refused to welcome them. Abraham, by contrast, leaps to his feet and runs towards them, bows to the ground and begs them to accept his hospitality.

He recognises the presence of God in these unexpected guests, bowing down before this presence. This man who, in earlier years, had often appeared to be self-serving, fearful for his own safety, and quite capable of deception now throws caution to the wind, welcoming strangers wholeheartedly, with refreshment freely offered.

Once, many years ago, I was a stranger myself in Hebron, and a local family offered me hospitality, generously sharing the little they had. I have never forgotten them. In their welcome I recognised the divine welcome. In their warmth I experienced something of the love of God.

The spirit of Abraham lives on in all who welcome the stranger with unconditional kindness. May it live on in us.

MARGARET SILF

No laughing matter

They said to him, 'Where is your wife Sarah?' And he said, 'There, in the tent.' Then one said, 'I will surely return to you in due season, and your wife Sarah shall have a son.' And Sarah was listening at the tent entrance behind him. Now Abraham and Sarah were old, advanced in age; it had ceased to be with Sarah after the manner of women. So Sarah laughed to herself... The Lord said to Abraham, 'Why did Sarah laugh and say, "Shall I indeed bear a child, now that I am old?" Is anything too wonderful for the Lord?'... Now Sarah said, 'God has brought laughter for me; everyone who hears will laugh with me.'

Sarai has also been given a new name, and, as Sarah, she has become the adopted daughter of God. Another promise is being made to her, through her husband Abraham in his conversation with the divine visitors. The strangers will return in due course, and when they do she will have a son.

The reading paints an image of this seriously post-menopausal woman listening in to the conversation from behind the entrance to the tent. I rather think that if I were ever to overhear such a promise at my time of life, I would react exactly as Sarah did.

We are not told directly how God reacted to her laughter. Not, it appears, with punishment or withdrawal of the promise of a child. Instead God challenges the laughter by asking whether anything is impossible for God. Sarah's laughter is the response of unbelief. She does not believe in miracles, and she has probably suffered quite a lot of mockery herself because of her infertility.

Yet there is a very moving sequel to this incident. When, aged 90, Sarah gives birth to Isaac, she rejoices with a very different kind of laughter, knowing that everyone who hears her story will laugh along with her in sheer joy that the impossible promise has been fulfilled. She has passed through and beyond her unbelief to a deeper level of faith. Her mocking laughter has been transformed into the laughter of happiness. Once she laughed at God in scorn. Now God laughs with her in her joy.

May God in whom all things are possible
transform our unbelief into ever-deeper faith.

MARGARET SILF

Abraham the negotiator

Then the Lord said, 'How great is the outcry against Sodom and Gomorrah and how very grave their sin!... Then Abraham came near and said, 'Will you indeed sweep away the righteous with the wicked? Suppose there are fifty righteous within the city; will you then sweep away the place and not forgive it for the fifty righteous who are in it?... Then he said, 'Oh, do not let my lord be angry if I speak just once more. Suppose ten are found there.' He answered, 'For the sake of ten I will not destroy it.' And the Lord went his way.

What a reversal! This is Abraham, who once devised cunning deceptions to secure his own safety. Abraham who once gambled his wife's freedom to save his own skin. Abraham who thought he knew better than God how to solve a problem. Now Abraham is the one standing up for justice and compassion. God, in the reading, is contemplating the destruction of Sodom and Gomorrah. The scene is reminiscent of the punishment raids inflicted in human history on whole communities who are believed to have harboured wrongdoers. It shocks us with its apparent injustice and lack of compassion. God, it seems, will likewise punish everyone in these troubled regions because of the extent of their sinfulness.

Whatever God's actual intentions may have been, Abraham leaps to the defence of the innocent and starts bargaining with God. The audacious gambler negotiates for compassion if just a few righteous men can be found, pushing the deal further and further until he has achieved agreement for clemency if a mere ten righteous people can be found in the sinful cities.

Perhaps this is a foretaste of the passion with which the father of future faiths will defend his multitudes of 'children'. Certainly it is a measure of how much this man has grown, spiritually, since God first intervened in his life. The apprentice in faith and trust now trusts in God absolutely to deliver justice with mercy, however serious the sin, however deep the depravity. There is a foreshadowing here, perhaps, of Jesus' later challenge to forgive 'seventy times seven' (Matthew 18:22, KJV).

May we learn from God to be wise in dispensing justice and generous in exercising compassion.

MARGARET SILF

The toxic force of revenge

The child grew and was weaned, and Abraham made a great feast on the day that Isaac was weaned. But Sarah saw the son of Hagar the Egyptian, who she had borne to Abraham, playing with her son Isaac. So she said to Abraham, 'Cast out this slave woman with her son, for the son of this slave woman shall not inherit along with my son Isaac'... So Abraham rose early in the morning and took bread and a skin of water and gave it to Hagar, putting it on her shoulder, along with the child, and sent her away. And she departed and wandered about in the wilderness of Beer-sheba.

The promised legitimate son, Isaac, has finally arrived and his weaning has been suitably celebrated. It sounds perfect – God's promise fulfilled. Sarah's sorrow is at an end. What could possibly mar such a happy ending? Enter the green-eyed monster. Sarah is consumed by jealousy. She cannot bear to see her son playing with little Ishmael, the son of Hagar, the child whose conception she herself had engineered.

Sarah cannot find it in her heart to forgive Hagar, even though it was her idea in the first place to bring Hagar and Abraham together. It had been her solution to the infertility problem, instead of trusting in God's promise. How hard it is, not just for Sarah, but for most of us, to trust the wisdom that holds all life in being, relying rather on our own flawed plans and projects. Sarah demands that Abraham cast out Hagar and her child, and Abraham does as he is told.

The poignancy of the final picture in today's reading is heart-rending, especially in the light of current conflicts in the world. Hagar is cast out into the desert with a little bread and water and a small child. She has been joined, in our times, by millions of other helpless victims of conflict.

The reading begins with an untroubled picture of two children playing happily together. It ends with the perennial question of inheritance that so often haunts human affairs. Whose child shall inherit this land?

An unforgiving heart leads to an unforgiving desert where humanity withers and dies.

MARGARET SILF

God rescues Ishmael

When the water in the skin was gone, she cast the child under one of the bushes... She said, 'Do not let me look on the death of the child'... The angel of God called to Hagar... 'Do not be afraid, for God has heard the voice of the boy where he is. Come, lift up the boy and hold him fast with your hand, for I will make a great nation of him.' Then God opened her eyes, and she saw a well of water. She went and filled the skin with water and gave the boy a drink.

The heartbreak expressed in this short passage, albeit in such an understated way, marks a kind of ground zero in the relationships between Abraham, Sarah, and Hagar. They are the victims of their own choices. Abraham went along with Sarah's plan to use Hagar as a surrogate, and Sarah found it impossible to let go of her resentment and sought revenge.

Today's reading focuses on the real victim of all this animosity: a small child, left in the desert under a bush by his heartbroken mother, because all means of sustaining his life are exhausted. She cannot bear to see her son die. At this point of utter desperation, God intervenes. Typically the divine rescue mission also includes another improbable promise. This child on the verge of death will, like Abraham, become the father of a great nation.

So Hagar is also blessed by God, who causes her eyes to open, so that she sees a well of water, the gift of life and hope. Her first response is an act of life-saving love. She fills the skin from the well, and gives her little boy a drink. In the course of time Jesus will also speak of himself as a source of living water, binding his own destiny with that of every abandoned child dying in the desert.

Divine justice is even-handed, as Friday's reading will confirm. God rescues Ishmael from an untimely death. God does not distinguish between children or draw dividing lines between nations. God's promise is unconditional and universal.

Divine justice is inseparable from divine compassion. May our human justice likewise always partner with human compassion.

MARGARET SILF

The sacrifice of Isaac

After these things God tested Abraham. He said to him, 'Abraham... Take your son, your only son Isaac, whom you love, and go to the land of Moriah and offer him there as a burnt offering on one of the mountains that I shall show you'... When they came to the place that God had shown him, Abraham built an altar there and laid the wood in order. He bound his son Isaac and laid him on the altar on top of the wood. Then Abraham reached out his hand and took the knife to kill his son.

The sacrifice of Isaac is certainly among the most problematic events in scripture. Again, a child is close to death – this time Isaac, Abraham's favoured, but second, son. God has personally required the sacrifice of Isaac, as a test of Abraham's faith. We are bound to ask what kind of 'father' imposes such a terrible requirement.

We are left with many questions. Abraham has challenged God with great persistence over the destruction of Sodom and Gomorrah, and yet he raises no protest when asked to kill his son. We have witnessed both his obedience and his wilfulness. On the one hand, he obeys God's command to leave home and head into the unknown; on the other hand, at the first sign of difficulty he insists on doing things his own way. He shows blind obedience, both to Sarah regarding the treatment of Hagar and to God in the sacrifice of his son.

The simple answer is that Abraham has reached a point, finally, of such complete trust in God's guidance that he is willing to entrust the life of the hapless Isaac into God's care. Simple answers, however, often conceal complex questions. Should we always conform to what we are told are divine rules or is it right sometimes to question them? Is total obedience always right? Should we be willing to sacrifice the family we love if a higher claim is made on our loyalty? Should one child be privileged over another in the same family based on the circumstances of their birth?

Whatever questions arise, the sacrifice of Isaac is clearly also, for Christians, understood to be a precursor of the sacrifice of Jesus.

Take all our questions, Lord, and help us to grow into the answers.

MARGARET SILF

God rescues Isaac

But the angel of the Lord called to him from heaven and said… 'Do not lay your hand on the boy or do anything to him, for now I know that you fear God, since you have not withheld your son, your only son, from me.' And Abraham looked up and saw a ram, caught in a thicket by its horns. Abraham went and took the ram and offered it up as a burnt offering instead of his son. So Abraham called that place 'The Lord will provide,' as it is said to this day, 'On the mount of the Lord it shall be provided.'

Just as God intervened to save Ishmael from imminent death in the desert, so now a divine intervention prevents the slaughter of Isaac. Whatever injustice in human terms separates these brothers, God's heart holds them both equally. Abraham's apparently unconditional faith is now vindicated by the angel's words, commending him for his willingness to sacrifice what he most loves, his own son. A substitute is even provided, in the form of a ram trapped by its horns in the undergrowth.

How might this extraordinary story speak to us today? We could simply regard it as one of the more difficult events in scripture, occurring at a time when human sacrifice was still practised and, most importantly, prefiguring the sacrifice of Jesus.

Yet there may be other searching questions to disturb us in this story. Abraham is willing to sacrifice what he most loves, because he trusts that God will turn this immense agony into a joy far greater, a joy that it is impossible to understand with our mortal minds. What matters most to us, and could we ever let it go?

Abraham, we might also reflect, has come to some understanding that the fullness of life is not constrained by our physical existence, and that whatever happens, Isaac's spirit will transcend the extinction of his physical presence. Can we also see beyond our limited physical lives to a life more true and full than anything we can imagine?

To do so does not lessen the anguish of sacrifice, both Abraham's and our own, but perhaps it lends meaning to the pain.

May our trust deepen and our fears lessen as we keep growing in faith.

MARGARET SILF

Homecoming

This is the length of Abraham's life, one hundred and seventy-five years. Abraham breathed his last and died in a good old age, old and full of years, and was gathered to his people. His sons Isaac and Ishmael buried him in the cave of Machpelah, in the field of Ephron son of Zohar the Hittite, east of Mamre, the field that Abraham purchased from the Hittites. There Abraham was buried with his wife Sarah. After the death of Abraham, God blessed his son Isaac. And Isaac settled at Beer-lahai-roi.

Abraham has come to the end of his long life. He is 'full of years' (v. 8). Sometimes we meet people ourselves who are full of years. The fullness of our years doesn't depend on the calendar but on how we have filled the years we have. Such fullness is often imprinted in lines and wrinkles, mapping a life marked by both joy and sorrow.

Today's reading is also a story of homecoming. Abraham once left all that was familiar to venture into the unknown under God's guidance. Now he returns to a very specific place of burial, where Sarah already lies. He is finally 'gathered to his people' (v. 8).

We learn that Abraham is buried by both his sons. The burial of a deceased parent was a legal obligation on their heirs. The fact that both sons bury their father could indicate a dispute over inheritance. Alternatively, observing this burial scene from such a distance in place and time, we might rather see two sons side by side, honouring their father's memory together, both heirs to God's promise, both called to become the progenitors of great nations.

The tree that has sprung from the root of Abraham's faithfulness has grown to fullness and fallen, leaving two strong and powerful branches. This ending is a new beginning. The fruits of this full life will bear the seeds of whole new chapters in the history of humankind in the form of two great peoples. The promise is made to us, too. All our lives have the potential to be the source of blessings upon the future.

May our lives be full and fruitful, and when we die
may we leave behind the seeds of blessing on those who follow after.

MARGARET SILF

Psalms 90—100

At the centre of our Bibles is the large song and prayer book we call the Psalms. It is for all God's people everywhere. And all of life finds voice there – the yearnings, hopes, suffering, joy, and frustrations that make up the experience of being alive, being human, and trying to understand and follow God in the midst of it all. Nothing is left out.

Over the next two weeks we will be reflecting on eleven of these psalms. They have in common a strong confidence in God's reigning presence, justice, and goodness in the world. They are songs of celebration for that reason. But their confidence in God does not mean life is easy. They are also songs of longing and yearning. For them, as for us, God's ways can be perplexing. We will hear them coming before God with their surprisingly blunt questions and very honest complaints. We can learn from this; God does not require us to be polite!

The psalms are not a private prayer book for us to pick and select from. There will be times when the psalm we are reading does not seem relevant to us. Its concerns and struggles are not our own. But there will be others for whom it is the only prayer they have. Christian praying is personal but never private. Have you noticed how, even when we are on our own, we pray '*Our* Father' not '*My* Father'? We are always praying with the whole of humanity, uniting ourselves with the circumstances, needs, hopes, and joys of people around the world we will never meet, but who are fellow pilgrims. And somewhere out there, others are praying for us.

Over these days let us allow the extracts from these songs and prayers to lead us into stories and journeys much bigger than our own and our life circumstances. With the psalms, we are praying and seeking God together, rejoicing with those who are rejoicing and weeping with those who are weeping (Romans 12:15). In this way all are welcomed, honoured, and given voice wherever God's people gather.

DAVID RUNCORN

How long?

Lord, you have been our dwelling place in all generations… From everlasting to everlasting you are God. You turn us back to dust… For we are consumed by your anger; by your wrath we are overwhelmed… For all our days pass away under your wrath… The days of our life are seventy years, or perhaps eighty, if we are strong… they are soon gone, and we fly away… So teach us to count our days that we may gain a wise heart. Turn, O Lord! How long?

At the centre of a psalm celebrating God as our compassionate, life-giving creator and secure dwelling place are disturbing verses about divine wrath. This is not, however, the contradiction that it first appears to be. God's wrath does not mean he has stopped being loving. God's wrathfulness is *because* of his love. He is angry *because* he cares, not because he has just lost his temper or rejected us.

God's wrath is his merciful resistance to all that denies his longing and good purposes in this world. A God who does not know wrath at the state of the world is not a God of justice or love. All that is not God must come face to face with this eventually.

The psalms take human accountability before God very seriously. They stress life's passing frailty and finitude – like the grass that in a hot climate only flourishes briefly before it dries up in the fierce heat of the sun. It may be that the root of human sin lies precisely in our unwillingness to live with the truth of that.

Life expectancy in that ancient world was not 70 years. Numbers are symbolic in the Bible. 'Seventy years' often referred to the length of the exile God's people were enduring. This gives us a context through which to understand the stress on wrath – overwhelming and divine anger – in this psalm. The people of Israel are in a far country, enduring painful estrangement from their land and their God.

There are people in the world today whose cry is also 'How long?' and who wait for a world that more clearly expresses God's unambiguous goodness and blessing. Today we make this cry with them and for them.

'How long, O Lord? How long?'

DAVID RUNCORN

Praying in the dust

You turn us back to dust… Have compassion on your servants! Satisfy us in the morning with your steadfast love, so that we may rejoice and be glad all our days. Make us glad as many days as you have afflicted us and as many years as we have seen evil… Let the favour of the Lord our God be upon us, and prosper for us the work of our hands – O prosper the work of our hands!

The Bible frequently stresses that we are creatures of the dust. This could easily leave us feeling that we are of no value. After all, what can you do with dust? To quote the meme: 'We come from the dust; we return to the dust. That is why I never dust. It might be someone I know.'

Another Hebrew word for the same truth is *hevel*. It occurs frequently in the book of Ecclesiastes, where it is commonly translated 'vanity'. This is misleading, as the word does not mean pride or meaninglessness. *Hevel* expresses the very texture of our existence – it is like the morning mist, tissue thin, a transitory, passing thing. It refers to the sheer fragility of this extraordinary gift of life.

This reminder keeps us grounded. It 'keeps us from hearing the gospel as a fairy story about a fantasy world where we might be free from the basic facts of life that constrain us in this present world' (Ellen F. Davis, *Proverbs, Ecclesiastes, and the Song of Songs*, Westiminster John Knox, 2004, p. 169).

Dust is not for despising. It is a source of wonder. Look what God creates out of it! The ancient storyteller could not have known what modern science has discovered. The dust out of which this world is formed is a gift of the entire universe and is constantly being renewed by it. The very substance of our being, the oxygen in our lungs, carbon in our muscles, calcium in our bones, iron in our blood, was all forged out of nuclear reactions and supernova explosions of stars long before the earth had come into being.

Who can make anything of dust? God can – and does so with endless creativity.

God, we are creatures of the dust –
work your creating wonders in us. Amen.

DAVID RUNCORN

God of many names

You who live in the shelter of the Most High, who abide in the shadow of the Almighty, will say to the Lord, 'My refuge and my fortress; my God, in whom I trust.' For he will deliver you from the snare of the hunter and from the deadly pestilence; he will cover you with his pinions, and under his wings you will find refuge; his faithfulness is a shield and defence... Those who love me, I will deliver; I will protect those who know my name. When they call to me, I will answer them; I will be with them in trouble.

The English translations do not make it clear, but in the opening two verses of this psalm, four ancient and holy Hebrew names for God are invoked: Elyon (Most High), Shaddai (the Almighty), Yahweh (Lord), and Elohim (God). In the scriptures, they each express aspects of divine character and purpose. For example, Shaddai is associated with judgement and justice; Yahweh is the name revealed to Moses at the burning bush. We cannot discuss this further now, but why not just read those opening verses aloud, inserting the original Hebrew names? Do not worry about getting the pronunciation right; just try it.

This is the psalmist's way of saying that life is encompassed by the whole revelation of God's character and actions. In Hebrew faith, to invoke the name of someone is more than to talk about or mention them. It is to make them effectively present. This is a psalm of robust confidence in the context of a world of frequent danger, hazards, evil, and opposition to true faith. To trust yourself to such a God is to know your true home and dwelling place and to have a refuge when you need it most.

Towards the end of the psalm, this confidence towards God and divine protection becomes so strong the voice tips over into the first person. God actually takes over the telling of it: 'Those who love me, I will deliver, protect, answer, be with them in trouble, rescue, honour, satisfy – and show my salvation.' Everything we need is here. What more is there to ask for?

God of many names, I trust you today. Amen.

DAVID RUNCORN

It is good

It is good to give thanks to the Lord, to sing praises to your name, O Most High… For you, O Lord, have made me glad by your work… How great are your works, O Lord… The stupid cannot understand this: though… all evildoers flourish, they are doomed to destruction forever… The righteous flourish like the palm tree… In old age they still produce fruit… showing that the Lord is upright; he is my rock, and there is no unrighteousness in him.

We live in a world very obsessed with knowing what is good for us. Advice is endless and everywhere on what to eat and drink, our physical and mental fitness, our daily lifestyle habits, and the secrets of good health. The psalmist's advice is simple and direct. What is good? 'To give thanks to the Lord' (v. 1). At the heart of human health is thanksgiving and praise.

The title of the psalm is 'A song for the sabbath day', so its context is the gathering of the people before their God on the sabbath. Three activities are found here, and they are the priorities whenever God's people meet for worship. First, God is praised and thanked for being God. Then testimonies and stories are shared of what God has been doing in our lives and how he has been real to us. Finally, we are here to learn. What is God teaching us through all this? What is deepening our understanding and strengthening our faith for the challenges life is bringing to us?

The goodness that brought creation into being still holds and sustains it. We can have confidence and trust in the future, says the psalmist. There is evil in the world, but it will not endure, for life without God is no life at all.

Such a joyful confidence amid a world like ours may well baffle many looking on. The psalmist bluntly mocks them as stupid – too dull to even consider the truth they are missing. Well, if this is smug faith, it is not for repeating. But if it is a way of robustly warning and calling out folly and evil in the world for what it is, it is surely good, too.

O God, thank you for being good. Amen.

DAVID RUNCORN

Girded with strength

The Lord is king; he is robed in majesty; the Lord is robed; he is girded with strength. He has established the world; it shall never be moved; your throne is established from of old; you are from everlasting. The floods have lifted up, O Lord, the floods have lifted up their voice; the floods lift up their roaring. More majestic than the thunders of mighty waters, more majestic than the waves of the sea, majestic on high is the Lord! Your decrees are very sure; holiness befits your house, O Lord, forevermore.

One way of reading this short psalm is to imagine it as an animated film with each part flowing in and out of the next and then back to the beginning on a continuous loop.

There is only one starting place. The Lord is king! God is enthroned, majestically robed – repeated twice. God is girded with strength. Girding is an old word meaning to encircle or fasten securely. This is the belt that gathers the robes in together. God's belt has the strength to gird everything securely in place.

The scene flows into what God has created, for that girding strength is what encircles and holds creation solidly in being, too. Nothing can threaten or shift it.

The scene changes again. Imagine a coastline on a stormy day. The sea is wild, the noise deafening. The psalmist imagines powerful creation rising and falling in praise, like those immense, rolling waves. But greater than creation's mightiest powers are the robes of God's majesty. We are back where we started. God is king and in that divine strength we are girded by something greater than everything else.

That this world is secure – 'established' – is a repeated theme in the psalms. It speaks reassuringly into the ancient anxiety that the world could tip back into the void of non-being from which it first came. But we read this psalm today from a perspective the psalmist could not have had and would never have thought possible. Humanity today has the potential to destroy itself and creation with it. If he was writing this psalm today, the psalmist would need an additional verse or two. What might he say?

Gird us in your strength, Almighty God. Amen.

DAVID RUNCORN

Deliver us

O Lord, you God of vengeance, you God of vengeance, shine forth! Rise up, O judge of the earth; give to the proud what they deserve… Can wicked rulers be allied with you, those who contrive mischief by statute? They band together against the life of the righteous and condemn the innocent to death. But the Lord has become my stronghold and my God the rock of my refuge. He will repay them for their iniquity and wipe them out for their wickedness; the Lord our God will wipe them out.

'God of vengeance… give to the proud what they deserve!' (vv. 1–2). The psalms are never afraid to call for divine payback on their enemies. But we will surely struggle with voicing such angry sentiments in our worship and prayer? Are we not supposed to love and forgive?

The problem is not that we get angry; it is anger that does not do what it is created for. Anger is there to be a force for good, resisting evil, purifying, transforming, and consuming what is *not* good. The psalms teach us that anger has an important place in our prayers. It must be given voice. What is its place in yours?

The psalmist points us to exactly the right place to take our anger: it is God who is judge. St Paul teaches: 'Beloved, never avenge yourselves, but leave room for the wrath of God, for it is written, "Vengeance is mine; I will repay, says the Lord"' (Romans 12:19).

There are people in the world today who know the need of this psalm only too well. It is their cry under the weight of the proud, violent, and arrogant. Those of us who have not had to endure such a world will struggle to imagine what it is like. But we pray this psalm with and for them.

Finally, though anger may be justified and right, it needs managing wisely. It is like a fire. If it simply rages out of control it will consume good and bad alike. We want evil wiped out. But we may pray that those caught up in that evil will finally be delivered from it and freed to live in goodness and justice.

O Lord, deliver us from evil. Amen.

DAVID RUNCORN

O come!

O come, let us sing to the Lord; let us make a joyful noise to the rock of our salvation! Let us come into his presence with thanksgiving; let us make a joyful noise to him with songs of praise!... O that today you would listen to his voice! Do not harden your hearts, as at Meribah, as on the day at Massah in the wilderness, when your ancestors tested me and put me to the proof, though they had seen my work. For forty years I loathed that generation and said, 'They are a people whose hearts go astray, and they do not regard my ways.' Therefore in my anger I swore, 'They shall not enter my rest.'

Some psalms address God. This one addresses us, calling us to worship and attentiveness. This psalm is the opening canticle in the traditional service of Morning Prayer, where it is called 'The Venite' – after the opening two words of the psalm in Latin, 'O come'. It calls the waking world to celebrate and remember the true source of its dawning: life starts here.

The canticle omits the end of the psalm, which contains a stern warning. It is the only part of the psalm quoted in the New Testament (Hebrews 3:7–11). In their wilderness wanderings, there were times when God's people became trapped in negativity, moaning, and bitterness. God feels the injustice and ingratitude of this. 'They had seen my work,' he exclaims (v. 9). They knew me better.

I notice how easily this happens on social media today. I used to enjoy a particular website. There was news, interesting articles, and lively debates about life and faith. But it became steadily taken over by complaining and criticism. Good news was mocked and excluded. The mood was more often judging and angry. Nothing was ever right. It was infecting me, too, and I was starting to talk like that, so I withdrew. Sometimes we have to leave.

The psalm tells us even God does. This is tough love. It is not forever, but God does not force himself on us. The psalm recalls us to the habit of remembering and celebrating what is good. Our health and salvation depends on it.

Forgive us our ingratitude and complaining, faithful God. Amen.

DAVID RUNCORN

Holy splendour

O sing to the Lord a new song; sing to the Lord, all the earth. Sing to the Lord; bless his name; tell of his salvation from day to day. Declare his glory among the nations, his marvellous works among all the peoples. For great is the Lord and greatly to be praised; he is to be revered above all gods… Worship the Lord in holy splendour; tremble before him, all the earth.

The well-known hymn 'O worship the Lord in the beauty of holiness' was inspired by verse 9 of this psalm. The translation used here speaks of 'holy splendour'. The verse continues: 'Tremble before him, all the earth.' Holiness is a fearful thing. This is the fear that is positively encouraged in the Bible, and that we are urged to learn. This is a fear that is wise, not unhealthy or morbid: 'The fear of the Lord is the beginning of wisdom' (Proverbs 9:10). It is not a cringing terror, but an appropriate awe and reverence that gives life its true shape and priority. It finds beautiful expression in lines from Frederick Faber's hymn, 'My God how wonderful thou art':

Oh how I fear thee living God,
with deepest tendr'est fears
and worship thee with trembling hope
and penitential tears.

A recent modernising of this hymn left out all mention of fear and trembling, implying it was not thought 'Christian'. This is profoundly mistaken. In C.S. Lewis' *The Lion, the Witch, and the Wardrobe*, Aslan is the name of a mysterious presence for whose coming all the faithful in Narnia long. There comes a moment when the children realise Aslan is a lion. 'Is he – quite safe?' one asks. 'I shall feel rather nervous about meeting a lion.' 'Safe?' comes the reply. 'Who said anything about safe? Course he isn't safe. But he's good. He's the King, I tell you.'

This holy fear in the presence of the beauty and splendour of God is 'pure' and 'enduring', says the psalmist (Psalm 19:9). It is a healthy fear. It is actually good for us, for it lays a secure foundation for our lives and guides our true priorities for good.

Oh, how I fear thee living God! Amen.

DAVID RUNCORN

The first Bible

Let the heavens be glad, and let the earth rejoice; let the sea roar and all that fills it; let the field exult and everything in it. Then shall all the trees of the forest sing for joy before the Lord, for he is coming, for he is coming to judge the earth. He will judge the world with righteousness and the peoples with his truth.

What is your relationship with the created world around us? We are much more aware, in our times, of our capacity to damage or even destroy our earthly home. Yet in the Bible creation is so much more than something we should be looking after better (though this is also clearly so). In the psalms the created world lives in joyful partnership with humanity, in the life of God. The universe is vibrantly alive in God. As today's extract illustrates, this is often expressed in a playful exuberance. Trees, fields, mountains, stars, rivers, and the waves of the sea dance, sing, clap, and shout for joy 'before the Lord' (v. 13).

This physical world is not inferior to the 'spiritual' world. Christian faith has been guilty of thinking like this. For the earliest Christian teachers, the universe was 'the first Bible' (Olivier Clément, *The Roots of Christian Mysticism*, New City, 1993, p. 27). It received its life from God billions of years before the first humans walked upon the earth. It has been a revelation of God's life and ways long before language existed and humanity tried to put all this wonder and meaning into words.

The contemplative monk Thomas Merton was reflecting the awareness of the psalms when he movingly wrote: 'There is, in all visible things, an invisible fecundity, a hidden wholeness. It rises up in wordless gentleness and flows out to me from the unseen roots of all created being' (*Raids on the Unspeakable*, New Directions, 1964, pp. 9–10).

'Consider the lilies,' said Jesus (Luke 12:27), who frequently taught using examples from the natural world. With the psalms, let us cultivate our partnership with the living world around us – learning to listen to it and to see and hear what it reveals of the unseen God.

With all created life, I shout for joy to the living God.

DAVID RUNCORN

Dazzling darkness

The Lord is king! Let the earth rejoice; let the many coastlands be glad! Clouds and thick darkness are all around him; righteousness and justice are the foundation of his throne. Fire goes before him and consumes his adversaries on every side… The mountains melt like wax before the Lord, before the Lord of all the earth… Light dawns for the righteous and joy for the upright in heart. Rejoice in the Lord, O you righteous, and give thanks to his holy name!

In ancient Israel the difference between idols and the true God is that you can see the idols. You cannot see the true God. 'Clouds and thick darkness are all around him,' says the psalmist (v. 2).

The 13th-century spiritual classic *The Cloud of Unknowing* is an extended reflection on this. The cloud is a metaphor for our inability to know God by our own finite reasoning, intellect, or imagination. After we have faithfully used up every word and image we can find to express our understanding of God, we must confess that God is so much more. It is inevitable that in drawing near to God all our ways of discerning and sensing will fail utterly. 'Truly, you are a God who hides himself,' says Isaiah (45:15). The apostle Paul writes of God who 'dwells in unapproachable light, whom no one has ever seen or can see' (1 Timothy 6:16); for him the darkness of faith comes from being blinded by a dazzling light, like trying to look at the sun. Elsewhere he uses another metaphor: 'Now we see only a reflection, as in a mirror' (1 Corinthians 13:12), but there will be a time when we shall see clearly.

This is called 'apophatic' faith. Sometimes word and imagination simply cannot express this holy mystery. The image of the thick dark cloud in Psalm 97 reminds us that this is beyond our grasp and control. We are being drawn to something utterly beyond us. We need reminding of this. Apophatic faith guards us against overfamiliarity, idolatry, and presumption. This cloud is not a loss of faith (though it can feel like that), but a deeper discovery; not emptiness, but the way to a greater fullness, in the wondrous, dazzling depths of a God who is beyond words and sight.

Lead us to faith beyond words and sight. Amen.

DAVID RUNCORN

Yet more

O sing to the Lord a new song, for he has done marvellous things. His right hand and his holy arm have gained him victory. The Lord has made known his victory; he has revealed his vindication in the sight of the nations... Break forth into joyous song and sing praises. Sing praises to the Lord with the lyre, with the lyre and the sound of melody. With trumpets and the sound of the horn make a joyful noise before the King, the Lord.

There is a new song to be sung, says the psalmist. There always is, for our God is the one who makes all things new (Revelation 21:5). On 16 September 1620, a boat called the *Mayflower* set sail from Plymouth for America – the New World. Among those on board were Christian pilgrims seeking a new home and freedom from relentless persecution they had known in England. On the quayside, pastor John Robinson urged his congregation to keep the faith with these well-known words: 'I am persuaded the Lord has more truth yet to break forth out of His Holy Word.'

'Breaking forth' suggests a dynamic, powerful energy at work that will not be confined or hemmed in. 'Yet more' is the insistence that there is always a newness to be revealed out of what is already given. That means our understanding is never exhausted, and in every time and place more will be breaking forth to guide the people of God in the challenges and questions they are facing. For that reason, Robinson called them to always be open and trusting in the face of the unknown. There will be more to be revealed. Christian faith is forward-looking. There is always a new song to be sung.

There is nothing wrong with the old songs. But new songs are needed wherever faith is being expressed in new contexts, is telling new stories, celebrating new discoveries, or has come to exciting fresh vision and understanding.

What new songs are you singing? What stories are you telling – whether large or small? You do not have to be a composer or musician. Just someone following the God who is making all things new. There is always more.

Does a song or hymn come to mind that you could sing?

DAVID RUNCORN

Our God reigns

The Lord is king; let the peoples tremble! He sits enthroned upon the cherubim; let the earth quake! The Lord is great in Zion; he is exalted over all the peoples… Mighty King, lover of justice, you have established equity; you have executed justice and righteousness in Jacob. Extol the Lord our God; worship at his footstool. Holy is he!

Psalms 93—99 are often called the 'enthronement psalms'. There is a constant, confident celebratory theme running through them because they believe 'our God reigns'.

Scholars always warn against trying to put a date to when particular psalms were written. We simply do not know their earliest context. But since these psalms so strongly rejoice in God's liberation, the saving of his people, and God's authority over all the nations of the world, it is easy to anticipate them being written and sung in a time of significant national deliverance.

The end of the great Babylonian empire was one such example. Israel's nation, land, holy city, and temple had been laid waste and the people forced into exile. But even the greatest earthly powers do not endure forever. At last, the all-dominant empire of Babylon was cast down. Its gods and armies were overcome. There were new songs to sing as God's people returned home at last. Our God reigns! At such times the sense of God's power and purposes, newly revealed in the world and to his people, would have been almost tangible.

In Israel's faith the defining story was their deliverance from Egypt. The psalmist recalls Moses and Aaron, as well as God's guiding through the wilderness. Samuel is also named (v. 6). He came much later, but he guided the nation through a spiritual crisis when faith was failing, leadership was compromised, and 'the word of the Lord was rare… visions were not widespread' (1 Samuel 3:1).

Remembering the stories of those who have gone before and how God guided and delivered them is the way the psalms seek to sustain faith in times when things appear otherwise. Do not lose hope. Despite all appearances, 'our God reigns!'

Reigning God, make your ways known in your world today. Amen.

DAVID RUNCORN

Where are you, God?

Moses and Aaron were among his priests, Samuel also was among those who called on his name. They cried to the Lord, and he answered them. He spoke to them in the pillar of cloud; they kept his decrees and the statutes that he gave them. O Lord our God, you answered them; you were a forgiving God to them but an avenger of their wrongdoings. Extol the Lord our God, and worship at his holy mountain, for the Lord our God is holy.

We have already noticed the confidence in these psalms that this world is secure under the reigning love of God. But it does not always feel like that, does it? The world can feel like a very disturbing and evil place. A great deal of evil and injustice has been going on, contradicting this secure picture of life. I want to say, 'But this does not feel true. Look at what is going on. Look at evil triumphing!'

The confidence of these psalms in God's security and protection is actually remarkable. In that ancient world the people of Israel were a tiny nation on a narrow strip of land that formed a bridge between three continents and the powerful nations that filled them. That made their land a continual battleground as competing empires fought for world dominance. Israel's stability and peace was dependent on backing the right superpower for protection. Their security could never be of their own making. So when psalms like this one claimed that God reigns securely over the world and establishes justice, they were expressing trusting faith in the midst of very vulnerable circumstances. They were claiming what was not always yet evident. Biblical faith is forward-looking in that sense. It anticipates what is promised but not yet revealed.

That is why these bold songs of confidence are found in among psalms of longing, protest, and bewilderment at the way things are. Then, as now, the world is often not what we thought was promised or what God surely intends.

The psalms call us to trust and faith, but they also call us to honesty when life seems to be contradicting what we were taught to believe.

God, whose reign brings security and justice – where are you right now?

DAVID RUNCORN

The discipline of celebration

Make a joyful noise to the Lord, all the earth. Serve the Lord with gladness; come into his presence with singing. Know that the Lord is God. It is he who made us, and we are his; we are his people and the sheep of his pasture. Enter his gates with thanksgiving and his courts with praise. Give thanks to him, bless his name. For the Lord is good; his steadfast love endures forever and his faithfulness to all generations.

Anyone can make a noise! You do not need particular skills to do it. When my children were young, we would sometimes get everything out on the floor and just make an immense crashing, chaotic noise with it all. It was such fun! When did you last just make a noise for the fun of it?

This psalm is a concluding response to the themes that have just gone before it. The mood is full of joyful, uninhibited gratitude, thanksgiving, and blessing. In Richard Foster's classic book *Celebration of Discipline* (Hodder and Stoughton, 1980), the final chapter is about the discipline of celebration. This is something we need to practise regularly until we have made a habit of it.

The spiritual discipline of examen is the practice of placing ourselves in God's presence at the end of the day or week and reviewing what has gone before, praying for the grace to discern God's acting in our lives. As we look back over it all, we seek where God has been real, where grace and mercy have touched us, and where we have known God's love and care. The mood is open and trusting. There is no condemnation.

Why not take some time to look back over the psalms we have been reading together. What has stood out? Where have been the gifts and challenges? Do this in gentleness and without forcing anything. Often what is the most significant may feel, initially, the least significant. Hold it with care and listen to it.

Then practise the discipline of celebration. Make a joyful noise! Let that sound break through our narrow preoccupations and open our hearts to the far greater story we are always part of.

Make a joyful noise to the Lord!

DAVID RUNCORN

Philippians

Philippi was a rich and cosmopolitan Roman city in Macedonia, in what is now north-eastern Greece. Its wealth was founded on plentiful deposits of gold nearby, as well as a seaport ten miles away, and its ethnically diverse citizens prided themselves on being Roman. The church there was founded when Paul, Silas, and Luke joined a group of 'God-fearing' women by the river to pray, and Lydia, a seller of luxury purple-dyed cloth, invited them to her home. You can read the story of their eventful stay in Acts 16:6–40.

This letter was written by Paul from prison, but we do not see any self-pity in it – rather he sees his imprisonment as an opportunity to spread the gospel more widely, including to his jailers (as he has previously done to a jailer in Philippi, Acts 16:19–34). In the letter he emphasises his love for this small but growing community, and his desire for them to express love for each other by seeking unity: not conformity, not even doctrinal 'purity', but a mutual affection based on their love for Jesus, who has sacrificed everything for them.

At the heart of the epistle Paul quotes what was probably an early church hymn about Jesus' incarnation, life, death, and resurrection, on which the hymn 'At the name of Jesus', written in 1870 by Caroline M. Noel, is based. The redemption brought about by Christ, it seems, is too great and mysterious to be expressed in anything but poetry. In response, Paul calls his hearers to strive for Christlikeness, not because we can earn our own salvation, but because God is at work in us to shape us for the kingdom and we need to respond to God's initiative.

Paul is also full of praise for this church in Philippi, especially for how they have supported him financially (see Philippians 4:15). While we should not be self-congratulatory, I wonder if your church could benefit from making a list of everything that is good about your life together?

VERONICA ZUNDEL

Nothing wasted

Paul and Timothy, servants of Christ Jesus, To all the saints in Christ Jesus who are in Philippi, with the bishops and deacons: Grace to you and peace from God our Father and the Lord Jesus Christ. I thank my God for every remembrance of you, always in every one of my prayers for all of you, praying with joy for your partnership in the gospel from the first day until now. I am confident of this, that the one who began a good work in you will continue to complete it until the day of Jesus Christ.

The first thing I noticed about the opening of this letter is that it is from Paul and his colleague Timothy together. This confirms for me the statement that the Mennonite missionary Alan Kreider used to make: 'Leadership is plural.' It is reinforced by the mention of the bishops and deacons. We should not think of a bishop here as someone who wears a fancy hat and lives in a palace. The Greek is *episkopos*, which simply means 'overseer', that is someone who had oversight of one or more congregations to make sure they were not going astray. Meanwhile deacons were the church's social workers (see Acts 6:1–6), who ensured that no one in the church was in need – although Stephen, one of the first deacons, also became the first martyr.

Second, I am struck by Paul's gratitude for his fellow believers. In every church we will find people we do not really get on with, but how often do we thank God for those with whom God has called us to worship and work? After a few years 'in the wilderness' church-wise, I am immensely thankful for the loving, welcoming, affectionate bunch of people I have now found myself among. It is a privilege to walk alongside them in my journey of faith.

Lastly, Paul reassures the Philippians that God is working in them and that no sacrifice or effort they make will be wasted. It is so easy to get discouraged and wonder, especially as we get older, whether our life has meant anything or had any impact on the world. This letter tells us that every life dedicated to Jesus makes a difference.

God who restores all things, finish in me what you have started. Amen.

VERONICA ZUNDEL

The problem of dodgy preachers

I want you to know, brothers and sisters, that what has happened to me has actually resulted in the progress of the gospel, so that it has become known throughout the whole imperial guard and to everyone else that my imprisonment is for Christ, and most of the brothers and sisters, having been made confident in the Lord by my imprisonment, dare to speak the word with greater boldness and without fear. Some proclaim Christ from envy and rivalry, but others from goodwill… What does it matter? Just this, that Christ is proclaimed in every way, whether out of false motives or true, and in that I rejoice.

Western Christians are sometimes quick to see persecution when all we are really experiencing is life in a secular society which gives rights – but not privileges – to all faiths. In other countries, the experience of Christians is often closer to that of Paul: imprisonment, torture, even death.

Paul, rather than lamenting his imprisoned state, saw it as creating new opportunities to spread the good news of Jesus. Even if some were taking advantage by preaching with bad motives or for monetary profit, it did not worry him too much so long as the name and life of Jesus was becoming better known. He was not concerned with his own reputation, but rather with that of God in Christ.

I wonder what he would make of today's televangelists making fortunes out of their followers or of politicians co-opting a caricature of Christian faith to gain political power? I think he might have a few choice words to say to them – but maybe not. Maybe he would rejoice that Christianity was still in the public discourse and use this opportunity to teach people a better, truer version of it?

We cannot tell; Paul is not here, and we are. How should we respond to versions of the gospel that seem to us to have little to do with Jesus? Should we 'call out' fake preachers?

'On that day many will say to me, "Lord, Lord, did we not prophesy in your name, and cast out demons in your name, and do many mighty works in your name?" Then I will declare to them, "I never knew you; go away from me, you who behave lawlessly"' (Matthew 7:22–23).

VERONICA ZUNDEL

Community, not conformity

If, then, there is any comfort in Christ, any consolation from love, any partnership in the Spirit, any tender affection and sympathy, make my joy complete: be of the same mind, having the same love, being in full accord and of one mind... Let the same mind be in you that was in Christ Jesus, who, though he existed in the form of God, did not regard equality with God as something to be grasped, but emptied himself, taking the form of a slave, assuming human likeness. And being found in appearance as a human, he humbled himself and became obedient to the point of death – even death on a cross.

Recently I watched a chilling documentary about an isolated Christian community in New Zealand that went seriously wrong. Members had to be utterly obedient to the founder, they wore 'modest' uniforms, which were – as is commonly the case – more restrictive for women than for men, and worst of all, sexual abuse of children was rife.

This aberration shows how we should never read 'Be of the same mind' (v. 2) as meaning we should aim for conformity. As 1 Corinthians 12 tells us, the body of Christ is made up of many different parts; the unity we seek does not cancel our diversity. Indeed, how could a body function at all if it did not have different organs?

Rather, 'Be of the same mind' is interpreted by the command just a few verses on: 'Let the same mind be in you that was in Christ Jesus' (v. 5). If you look at Jesus' teaching and ministry, he was different with each different person or group that he related to, yet there was a consistency in his actions and words, the theme throughout being self-giving love.

These words are poetry, set out as such in the Bible. They are probably an early hymn, the rest of which continues in tomorrow's reading. What this part describes is what is called Jesus' *kenosis*, or self-emptying, his choice to be completely immersed in human experience, right to the death we all share. He is our example.

'For you know the generous act of our Lord Jesus Christ, that though he was rich, yet for your sakes he became poor' (2 Corinthians 8:9).

VERONICA ZUNDEL

The greatest story

Therefore God exalted him even more highly and gave him the name that is above every other name, so that at the name given to Jesus every knee should bend, in heaven and on earth and under the earth, and every tongue should confess that Jesus Christ is Lord, to the glory of God the Father. Therefore, my beloved, just as you have always obeyed me, not only in my presence but much more now in my absence, work on your own salvation with fear and trembling, for it is God who is at work in you, enabling you both to will and to work for his good pleasure.

I have been taking an online course in narrative poetry – poems that tell a story, however obliquely or out of order. I chose this because I have noticed that the poems of mine that are most likely to win prizes or be published are those that tell stories.

Paul's favourite word in his epistles is 'therefore', which suggests that Paul is pursuing arguments rather than telling a story. However, here he is clearly telling a story, that of Jesus' death and resurrection, helped by quoting what may have been a hymn (again, the biblical text up to 'Father' is set out in verse). The first 'Therefore' tells us why Jesus has been raised to the highest position, because he was willing to descend to the lowest depths, as we saw yesterday. The second 'Therefore' calls out our response to that story.

That response is not necessarily what many Christians these days would expect. We might be anticipating Paul to write, 'Therefore, accept the grace God has extended to you in Christ, put your faith in him, and you will find salvation.' But instead we get: 'Work on your own salvation with fear and trembling' (v. 12). Faith is not about just lying back and believing – it is about active cooperation with the work of God's kingdom. Of course, this is impossible without 'God… at work in you, enabling you both to will and to work' (v. 13). It is a paradox, summed up in St Augustine's words: 'Pray as if everything depends on God. Work as if everything depends on you.'

'At the name of Jesus, Every knee shall bow' (Caroline M. Noel, 1817–77).

VERONICA ZUNDEL

Dogs or children?

Beware of the dogs, beware of the evil workers, beware of those who mutilate the flesh! For it is we who are the circumcision, who worship in the Spirit of God and boast in Christ Jesus and have no confidence in the flesh… If anyone else has reason to be confident in the flesh, I have more: circumcised on the eighth day, a member of the people of Israel, of the tribe of Benjamin, a Hebrew born of Hebrews; as to the law, a Pharisee; as to zeal, a persecutor of the church; as to righteousness under the law, blameless. Yet whatever gains I had, these I have come to regard as loss because of Christ… For his sake I have suffered the loss of all things, and I regard them as rubbish, in order that I may gain Christ.

Now here is another surprise. 'Dogs' was a term used by Jews to insult Gentiles, who were outside God's covenant. You can see it in the incident of the Gentile woman who begged Jesus to heal her daughter (Mark 7:24–30; Matthew 15:21–28), and who turns around his refusal, claiming: 'Sir, even the dogs under the table eat the children's crumbs' (Mark 7:28).

Yet here, Paul is using that same insult to warn against the pious Jews themselves, those who had come to follow Jesus yet were insisting that Gentile believers be circumcised and follow the Jewish law. He does not mince his words: such traditional practice is 'mutilation' and a work of evil. Quite apart from anything else, it drives a wedge between men and women: circumcision applies only to men, and women gain salvation by belonging to a circumcised man, while baptism is open to both sexes. This is highlighted in Galatians 3:27–29, where baptism replaces circumcision as a sign which applies equally to Jew and Gentile, slave and free, man and woman.

For Paul, true circumcision is the 'circumcision of the heart' (Deuteronomy 30:6) and for the sake of knowing Christ, he is now willing to throw away all the advantages he had as a Jewish rabbi. Here is another interesting word: the Greek word translated as 'rubbish' actually means 'excrement', but no translators dare to translate it literally!

What would you throw, or what have you thrown, away for Christ?

VERONICA ZUNDEL

Winning the prize

Not that I have already obtained this or have already reached the goal, but I press on to lay hold of that for which Christ has laid hold of me. Brothers and sisters, I do not consider that I have laid hold of it, but one thing I have laid hold of: forgetting what lies behind and straining forward to what lies ahead, I press on towards the goal, towards the prize of the heavenly call of God in Christ Jesus. Let those of us, then, who are mature think this way, and if you think differently about anything, this, too, God will reveal to you. Only let us hold fast to what we have attained.

Sadly, at school I was always the last kid to be picked for a team in 'games'. I could barely throw a ball, let alone catch it. What about you?

Paul here, as elsewhere, picks a metaphor from athletics to express his thoughts about the Christian life. It is like a race, but not one in which the aim is to beat the others. Rather, it is a race in which we are to fix our eyes on the finishing line, without making any judgemental comparisons between how we are doing and how others are. The trick is to not look back at past failures, but to look forward to our prize: being fully in the image of Jesus, being Christlike. This is in fact a race in which all runners win prizes, but only by completing the race.

If we are going to win a prize just for sticking to the race, why try harder? Well, we should not push metaphors too far, but remember what we read two days ago: 'Work on your own salvation… for it is God who works in you' (2:12–13). Paul says something similar here: 'I press on to make it my own, because Christ Jesus has made me his own' (3:12, ESV). Our persistence is our response to God's persistence in seeking and finding us when we were lost. Once again, Paul appeals to his hearers to be 'of the same mind' – not all agreeing about everything, but all agreeing to seek 'the mind of the Spirit' on contentious issues.

'For the letter kills, but the Spirit gives life' (2 Corinthians 3:6).

VERONICA ZUNDEL

Seek the truth

I urge Euodia and I urge Syntyche to be of the same mind in the Lord. Yes, and I ask you also, my loyal companion, help these women, for they have struggled beside me in the work of the gospel… Let your gentleness be known to everyone… Do not be anxious about anything, but in everything by prayer and supplication with thanksgiving let your requests be made known to God. And the peace of God, which surpasses all understanding, will guard your hearts and your minds in Christ Jesus. Finally, brothers and sisters, whatever is true, whatever is honourable, whatever is just, whatever is pure, whatever is pleasing, whatever is commendable, if there is any excellence and if there is anything worthy of praise, think about these things.

In a local church founded by a wealthy businesswoman, it is unsurprising that women played a prominent role as co-workers in the gospel (see also Romans 16:1–16). I doubt if their dispute was about the flower rota! But when those who have been used to having no power and no voice suddenly get key roles in ministry, it is likely that they might clash with each other.

There it is again: that plea to be 'of the same mind' (v. 2). I think this is more about helping these women focus on the will of God together, rather than reaching a negotiated truce. Gentleness is the key, but note that Paul requires this not only of women but of men, too. Anxiety is the enemy of peace, both inner peace and peace between people, and Paul encourages us to bring our anxieties to God and leave them there.

Finally, rather than obsessing about the state of the world or perceived offences by others, we are to focus on whatever we can see that is good. This is not all about pictures of fluffy bunnies and baskets of flowers, though. The first word in the list is 'true'. Without being clear-eyed about truth, we cannot have an honest view of everything else that is good in the world.

'Do all things without murmuring and arguing, so that you may be blameless and innocent, children of God without blemish in the midst of a crooked and perverse generation, in which you shine like stars in the world' (Philippians 2:14–15).

VERONICA ZUNDEL

Mountains and hills

Throughout history, mountains, hills, and high places generally have carried a numinous quality; and it was not only the Jewish and Christian faiths which frequently established their centres of worship on them. We will see something of this quality at work in a number of the reflections that follow; in particular, perhaps, the account in John 4 of Jesus' meeting with the woman at the well in Samaria.

In these passages, we shall explore a number of occasions when God's people, from Old Testament times and into the New, encountered God on a mountain. Christ himself frequently withdrew to the mountains to pray. Such a quiet and rarified atmosphere as a mountain would provide must have helped intensify those precious times of communion with God, away from the continuous hurly-burly and distractions of the ever-present crowd. For Jesus, these times of retreat were often critical, as they often preceded important decisions, like the direction his ministry was to take, and the choosing of those disciples – apostles – who were to be his closest friends and companions in ministry.

Yet we need to take care, because it is possible to romanticise all this. Without doubt mountaintops offer a wonderful view, but such locations offer the possibility of so much more. Several of our passages deal with soul-searing, life-changing encounters with God, as seen most clearly in such passages as Exodus 3 (Moses' experience of the burning bush), Exodus 19 (Moses' ascent of Mount Sinai), and 1 Kings 19 (Elijah's encounter with God in 'a sound of sheer silence' on Mount Horeb).

Sometimes the mountains we consider appear symbolically. We will consider the fearful warning sounded by the prophet Joel of Mount Zion concerning the coming day of the Lord; while Isaiah presents a graphic picture of the same mountain as the site of a 'feast of rich food' – a much more positive image of the apocalyptic future. There is no right or wrong here; both perspectives are essential.

The sequence of passages chosen ranges from Noah and his family finding safety on Mount Ararat after the flood, to the author of the book of Hebrews' vision of Mount Zion and the heavenly Jerusalem.

BARBARA MOSSE

Refuge and safety

At the end of one hundred and fifty days the waters had abated… the ark came to rest on the mountains of Ararat. The waters continued to abate until the tenth month… the tops of the mountains appeared. At the end of forty days Noah opened the window of the ark… and sent out the raven… Then he sent out the dove… but the dove found no place to set its foot, and it returned to him in the ark… He waited another seven days… and the dove came back to him in the evening, and there in its beak was a freshly plucked olive leaf; so Noah knew that the waters had subsided from the earth.

As the flood begins to subside, the ark comes to rest on the mountains of Ararat. After so long pent up in such a small space, there must have been the temptation to rush out of the ark, but Noah acts otherwise. What follows for him and his family is a careful, measured, well-tested return to the beginnings of a new life on a newly washed earth.

When Noah built the ark, he was obeying the direct instructions God was giving him. This gave rise to the derision of his family and neighbours, who saw no signs of the coming deluge. But what happens here at this point when the flood has abated? There is no heavenly voice; instead, Noah uses his God-given common sense. With the resources he has to hand (a raven and a dove), he uses a gradual, step-by-step process to determine whether or not there is enough dry land to leave the ark safely. When the dove is finally sent out and does not return (v. 12), Noah knows it is safe to disembark.

When we pray for guidance, we sometimes expect it to come in spectacular ways: floodlit, possibly with bells and whistles attached. But the guidance that Noah received after the flood was not of this type; rather it came from close observation of what was happening around him, patience, and the use of his own common sense.

Dear Lord, help us to be alert to your guidance in whatever forms you send it, whether through directly 'hearing' your voice or through the use of our God-given common sense. Amen.

BARBARA MOSSE

On holy ground

Moses was keeping the flock of his father-in-law Jethro... he led his flock beyond the wilderness and came to Mount Horeb, the mountain of God. There the angel of the Lord appeared to him in a flame of fire out of a bush; he looked, and the bush was blazing, yet it was not consumed... When the Lord saw that he had turned aside to see, God called to him out of the bush, 'Moses, Moses!' And he said, 'Here I am.' Then he said, 'Come no closer! Remove the sandals from your feet, for the place on which you are standing is holy ground... I am the God of your father, the God of Abraham, the God of Isaac, and the God of Jacob.' And Moses hid his face, for he was afraid to look at God.

The sense of holiness within this passage is clear, in spite of the fact that Moses is engaged in an everyday task: tending the flock of his father-in-law Jethro. But this normal routine for Moses was to turn into something extraordinary. We are at Horeb, the mountain of God, and it is here that Moses sees a bush which is burning but not consumed. If Moses had simply walked on by things might well have ended here. But he chose to stop, turn aside, and look – and God spoke.

If we read on, we will learn of the great task God lays on Moses' shoulders; for now, let us stay with this idea of turning aside and looking. Today life moves at such a pace, and we tend to rush through our days in an attempt to keep up. Who knows how many 'burning bushes' we miss in the process? God plants burning bushes all around us, hidden in plain sight within our normal everyday pattern of life. But we will only hear God's voice if we stop, breathe deeply, open our inner ears and eyes, and listen.

Lord Jesus, help us to journey through our days with mindful attentiveness. Help us to a place of inner stillness, alert and alive to the presence of God which is in us and all around us. Help us to know that, wherever we are, we are standing on holy ground. Amen.

BARBARA MOSSE

In darkness and fire

On the morning of the third day there was thunder and lightning, as well as a thick cloud on the mountain, and a blast of a trumpet so loud that all the people who were in the camp trembled. Moses brought the people out of the camp to meet God. They took their stand at the foot of the mountain. Now all of Mount Sinai was wrapped in smoke, because the Lord had descended upon it in fire; the smoke went up like the smoke of a kiln, while the whole mountain shook violently… When all the people witnessed the thunder and lightning, the sound of the trumpet, and the mountain smoking, they were afraid… and said to Moses, 'You speak to us, and we will listen, but do not let God speak to us, lest we die.' Moses said to the people, 'Do not be afraid…' Then the people stood at a distance, while Moses drew near to the thick darkness where God was.

This theophany (visible manifestation of God), where God appears to Moses, sets the scene for the giving of the ten commandments. But although Moses is the only one to ascend the mountain, the whole people of Israel witness the proceedings from its foot. And it is quite a display: thunder and lightning, cloud and fire, and a trumpet blast so loud that the people are terrified.

The closing words of today's passage, which writes of 'the thick darkness where God was', may surprise us, when we are more used to considering God as light. We may feel unsettled, but the strangeness is only superficial. 'Darkness' imagery tends to convey the awesome mystery, the ultimate 'otherness' of God, who lies beyond the limit of our human senses; and it offers a helpful corrective to our tendency to over-domesticate God.

Perhaps we shouldn't get too comfortable with picturesque and beautiful imagery! In the Bible mountains tend to be challenging places of encounter with God, where the ordinariness of human experience encounters the awesomeness and unpredictability of the holy. Tomorrow, we shall encounter God on Mount Horeb in a very different, but equally transformative, guise.

Mysterious God, whose darkness guides more surely than our light;
may we trust you in cloud and in sunlight, until we know
as we are fully known. Amen.

BARBARA MOSSE

A sound of sheer silence

Then the word of the Lord came to him, saying, 'What are you doing here, Elijah?' He answered, 'I have been very zealous for the Lord, the God of hosts, for the Israelites have forsaken your covenant… I alone am left, and they are seeking my life, to take it away.' [God] said, 'Go out and stand on the mountain before the Lord…' Now there was a great wind… but the Lord was not in the wind, and after the wind an earthquake… and after the earthquake a fire… and after the fire a sound of sheer silence. When Elijah heard it, he wrapped his face in his mantle and went out and stood at the entrance to the cave. Then there came a voice to him that said… 'Go, return on your way to the wilderness of Damascus.'

As we join Elijah, he has fled to Mount Horeb from the wrath of Queen Jezebel after he had killed all her prophets, and there is more than a suggestion of 'It's not fair!' about his attitude. Elijah has important lessons to learn here before he is ready for the next task God has for him.

One of those lessons is the realisation that God has scant sympathy with 'It's not fair.' Twice God asks the question 'What are you doing here, Elijah?' (once in this abridged extract); twice God ignores Elijah's complaint but gives him an instruction: first, to stand out on the mountain before the Lord, and second, to accept God's instructions and return to the place he was fleeing from.

So what enabled Elijah to literally 'turn around'? I suggest it was the nature of the epiphany he experienced when he stood on the mountain, waiting for the Lord to pass by. And so came the wind, the earthquake, and the fire – but the Lord wasn't in any of them. Only in the 'sound of sheer silence' did Elijah become quiet and attentive enough to begin to hear what God was asking of him.

Have you ever tried taking your 'It's not fair!' feelings to God? If so, how do you feel God responded?

BARBARA MOSSE

God's eternity and human frailty

Lord, you have been our dwelling place in all generations. Before the mountains were brought forth, or ever you had formed the earth and the world, from everlasting to everlasting you are God. You turn us back to dust and say, 'Turn back, you mortals.' For a thousand years in your sight are like yesterday when it is past or like a watch in the night. You sweep them away; they are like a dream, like grass that is renewed in the morning; in the morning it flourishes and is renewed; in the evening it fades and withers... The days of our life are seventy years, or perhaps eighty, if we are strong... So teach us to count our days, that we may gain a wise heart.

Have you ever looked at a mountain – any mountain – and marvelled at the unimaginable stretches of time and the mysteries of the creative process that were needed to bring it into being? Our minds may not be able to fully grasp the enormity and scope of God's loving, creative action, but Psalm 90 reassures us that God's creative, nurturing presence remains steadfastly with us, from the darkness of the pre-creation past to the equally unimaginable consummation in the future.

And against the promise of God's constant presence, the reality of our human frailty is laid bare; we are here in this life for nothing more than a blink of God's eye. But in this there is another ground for reassurance. How often do we hear people fret because they have to leave tasks unfinished, because despite their best efforts, there are not enough hours in the day (or years in a lifetime)? Psalm 90 tells us that full completion in our own short time span is not to be expected.

The theologian Reinhold Niebuhr (1892–1971) said: 'Nothing that is worth doing can be achieved in our lifetime; therefore we must be saved by hope. Nothing which is true or beautiful or good makes complete sense in any immediate context of history; therefore we must be saved by faith. Nothing we do, however virtuous, can be accomplished alone; therefore we are saved by love' (*The Irony of American History*, Scribner, 1952, p. 63).

Lord, you have been our dwelling place in all generations.
So teach us to count our days that we may gain a wise heart. Amen.

BARBARA MOSSE

The Lord is with us

Those who trust in the Lord are like Mount Zion, which cannot be moved but abides forever. As the mountains surround Jerusalem, so the Lord surrounds his people from this time on and forevermore. For the sceptre of wickedness shall not rest on the land allotted to the righteous, so that the righteous might not stretch out their hands to do wrong. Do good, O Lord, to those who are good and to those who are upright in their hearts. But those who turn aside to their own crooked ways, the Lord will lead away with evildoers. Peace be upon Israel!

While relevant in their own time, the words of Psalm 125 still have much to say to us today. A glance at any page of any newspaper will reveal a pervasive culture of insatiable greed and violence. The climate of fear, uncertainty, and anxiety seems to be worldwide. The past centuries telescope together as 'the righteous' in our world seek to work for good, as opposed to those who 'turn aside to their own crooked ways' (v. 5).

Has anything really changed in the intervening centuries? Maybe not, to our limited vision. But the Lord here calls on us to remember that our vision is limited, and we cannot begin to grasp the depth and timescale at which God works. So where should our focus be? We are urged to trust in the Lord, and are told that those who do so 'are like Mount Zion, which cannot be moved, but abides forever' (v. 1).

Mount Zion is a powerful symbol, whose meaning tends to shift through scripture. The actual mount is a hill just outside Jerusalem, but symbolically it stands for Jerusalem itself, and later for the mount on which the temple was built. In this passage the symbolic meaning has shifted again: it is those who trust who are like Mount Zion, in their solid, rock-like qualities, and their determination not to be moved. Then the Lord himself is identified with the mountains around Jerusalem (of which Mount Zion is one), surrounding his people and keeping them safe in him forever.

Strengthen us, O Lord, when our faith is weak and we find it hard to trust. Help us look to the promise of your eternal presence, guiding and holding us through all that life brings. Amen.

BARBARA MOSSE

God's holy mountain (1)

Blow the trumpet in Zion; sound the alarm on my holy mountain! Let all the inhabitants of the land tremble, for the day of the Lord is coming, it is near – a day of darkness and gloom, a day of clouds and thick darkness! Like blackness spread upon the mountains, a great and powerful army comes; their like has never been from of old, nor will be again after them in ages to come... Yet even now, says the Lord, return to me with all your heart, with fasting, with weeping, and with mourning; rend your hearts and not your clothing. Return to the Lord your God, for he is gracious and merciful, slow to anger, abounding in steadfast love, and relenting from punishment.

Joel's prophecy at this point is an ominous one, filling his hearers with a sense of fear and foreboding. The mountain in question here is God's holy mountain of Zion, from where the alarm will sound to announce the coming day of the Lord. The first two verses seem to offer anything but good news: God's people have rebelled and strayed so far from God's ways that a drastic response – described in the form of a powerful attacking army – is called for. The theologian William Lloyd Allen observes that God, humanity, and the wider creation are inextricably linked, and that the alarm is sounded because things have got seriously out of balance.

The alarm still sounds today. To a greater or lesser degree, we all experience the effects of climate change, a growing ecological crisis, and the devastating effects of human greed and selfishness. We cannot know what the outcome will be or how it will come about, but it should come as no surprise that this text provides one of the key readings for Ash Wednesday. A complete turnaround is needed, a sincere repentance for the part we have played in creation's imbalance and a deep, heartfelt returning to God with our whole being. This is where our hope lies: in a reordering of ourselves and our priorities and a return to the source of our life and being.

Dear Lord, help us to make each day an Ash Wednesday, and so renew our relationships with you, each other, and our world. Amen.

BARBARA MOSSE

God's holy mountain (2)

On this mountain the Lord of hosts will make for all peoples a feast of rich food, a feast of well-aged wines, of rich food filled with marrow, of well-aged wines strained clear. And he will destroy on this mountain the shroud that is cast over all peoples… he will swallow up death forever. Then the Lord God will wipe away the tears from all faces, and the disgrace of his people he will take away from all the earth… It will be said on that day, 'See, this is our God… This is the Lord for whom we have waited; let us be glad and rejoice in his salvation.' For the hand of the Lord will rest on this mountain.

Today we are back on God's holy mountain again, but what a different picture is painted here! Yesterday's passage was full of gloom and dire warnings of judgement; today's text directs our glance forward into God's future and is full of light and promise. As we focus today on Isaiah's prophecy of a future full of healing and wholeness, it is important that we do not forget the other picture. We need to embrace the message of judgement *before* we welcome the promise and the hope; they belong together as two sides of the same coin.

The promises here are breathtaking. First is the promise of a feast for *all* peoples; the 'shroud' and the 'sheet' which have been cast over all nations, causing enmity and division, will be destroyed forever. And the food! Not just any food and just enough, but rich food filled with marrow and well-aged wines, in abundance. Sorrow and death will be experiences consigned to the past, having no place in God's kingdom.

We look at our world today with its seemingly intractable problems – the displacement of millions through war, famine, injustice, the list goes on. This prophecy promises such a transformation that our minds struggle to grasp it. Humanly, it is surely impossible. But we have what Isaiah's original hearers didn't have – the knowledge of Jesus' resurrection from the dead – and it is in this glorious truth that our faith and our hope rest.

Help us, Lord, to so know you in your death and resurrection that we may look 'beyond the veil' in hope and trust. Amen.

BARBARA MOSSE

In spirit and in truth

[Jesus] had to go through Samaria… Jacob's well was there, and Jesus, tired out by his journey, was sitting by the well. It was about noon. A Samaritan woman came to draw water, and Jesus said to her, 'Give me a drink'… The Samaritan woman said to him, 'How is it that you, a Jew, ask a drink of me, a woman of Samaria?' (Jews do not share things in common with Samaritans.)… The woman said to him… 'Our ancestors worshipped on this mountain, but you say that the place where people must worship is in Jerusalem.' Jesus said to her, 'Woman, believe me, the hour is coming when you will worship the Father neither on this mountain nor in Jerusalem… But the hour is coming and is now here when the true worshippers will worship the Father in spirit and truth, for the Father seeks such as these to worship him. God is spirit, and those who worship him must worship in spirit and truth.'

Whole books have been written about this many-stranded encounter between Jesus and the Samaritan woman, and we will focus on just one of those strands today. The first few verses set the scene. Jesus, weary from his journey, rests by Jacob's well. When the Samaritan woman approaches, he breaks several societal taboos at once.

First, he asks a woman directly for help, a thing no self-respecting Israelite man would do – Jesus' disciples 'were astonished that he was speaking with a woman' (v. 27). Second, to make matters worse, she was a Samaritan. The intense rivalry between the Samaritans and the Israelite people began around 200BC, over the correct siting for the centre of worship: the Samaritans opting for Mount Gerazim, the Israelites for Jerusalem.

As the woman grows in confidence through Jesus' teaching and leading, she goes straight to the heart of the matter – 'Our ancestors worshipped on this mountain, but you say…' (v. 20). Jesus resists the either/or dilemma and moves the woman's understanding on with an answer that transcends both: the time will come, says Jesus, when true worship will take place neither on this mountain nor in Jerusalem, but will seek the Father in spirit and truth.

Has this teaching got anything to say about our own attachment to particular places or ways of worship?

BARBARA MOSSE

Sermon on the mount

'You have heard that it was said, "An eye for an eye and a tooth for a tooth." But I say to you: Do not resist an evildoer. But if anyone strikes you on the right cheek, turn the other also, and if anyone wants to sue you and take your shirt, give your coat as well… You have heard that it was said, "You shall love your neighbour and hate your enemy." But I say to you: Love your enemies and pray for those who persecute you, so that you may be children of your Father in heaven.'

The sermon on the mount occupies three chapters of Matthew's gospel. We focus today on that section which concerns Jesus' teaching on forgiveness.

Matthew's Jesus makes the love of God and one's neighbour the foundational requirement from which everything else follows. And he is not talking about a vague, generalised love, but one targeted not only at those whom we dislike or find irritating, but also (and especially) at those whom we find hardest to love and forgive: our enemies and persecutors.

For most of us, forgiveness does not come easily. In my own experience forgiveness tends to be more of a process – sometimes taking place over many years – than an instant act. But there may be times when Christ asks for the instant response, as in the experience of Corrie ten Boom. She was a Dutch watchmaker who sheltered Jews during World War II. She was betrayed and imprisoned in Ravensbruck but survived the Holocaust. In 1947, when in Germany, she was approached by a prison guard who had been complicit in her sister Betsie's death. Holding out his hand, he asked for her forgiveness. She was almost overcome by feelings of anger and repugnance, but she nevertheless took his hand. She describes what happened next: 'For a long moment we grasped each other's hands, the former guard and the former prisoner. I had never known God's love so intensely as I did then' (Corrie ten Boom, *Tramp for the Lord*, Hodder & Stoughton, 1975, pp. 217–18).

Heavenly Father, when we struggle with personal hurt and grudges, help us to be willing to embrace Christ's teaching on forgiveness. If even that feels too hard, help us to be willing to be willing. In Jesus' name. Amen.

BARBARA MOSSE

Mount of betrayal

They went to a place called Gethsemane, and he said to his disciples, 'Sit here while I pray.' He took with him Peter and James and John and began to be distressed and agitated. And he said to them, 'My soul is deeply grieved, even to death; remain here, and keep awake.' And going a little farther, he... said, 'Abba, Father, for you all things are possible; remove this cup from me, yet not what I want but what you want.' He came and found them sleeping, and he said to Peter, 'Simon, are you asleep?... Keep awake and pray that you may not come into the time of trial; the spirit indeed is willing, but the flesh is weak.' And again he went away and prayed... And once more he... found them sleeping... He came a third time and said to them, 'Are you still sleeping and taking your rest? Enough! The hour has come; the Son of Man is betrayed into the hands of sinners.'

Gethsemane was a quiet garden just outside the walls of Jerusalem, at the foot of the Mount of Olives. Jesus retreated to the garden to pray, and took with him Peter, James, and John.

Mark provides two areas of focus for our reflections. The first concerns Christ and his mental state, compounded by his betrayal by Judas, as he sees the cross approaching. We are given a harrowing description of Jesus' mental and spiritual agony as he prays to his Father 'that, if it were possible, the hour might pass from him' (v. 35). But even at this point of supreme suffering, he chooses to submit himself to God's will. Jesus' suffering is real, and his experience offered a powerful corrective to those whose expectations of a Messiah were of an all-powerful, all-conquering hero.

The second area focuses on the reactions of the disciples. When urged three times by Jesus to stay awake, they fell asleep each time. Would we have done that? But before we criticise them, perhaps we should remind ourselves that human beings have a tendency to switch off if another's suffering gets too acute.

How do you identify with Christ here – and with the disciples?

BARBARA MOSSE

Time with God

Now during those days he went out to the mountain to pray, and he spent the night in prayer to God. And when day came, he called his disciples and chose twelve of them, whom he also named apostles... He came down with them and stood on a level place with a great crowd of his disciples and a great multitude of people from all Judea, Jerusalem, and the coast of Tyre and Sidon. They had come to hear him and to be healed of their diseases, and those who were troubled with unclean spirits were cured. And everyone in the crowd was trying to touch him, for power came out from him and healed all of them.

It may have been John Wesley who said, 'I'm going to be so busy today that I can't afford to spend less than four hours in prayer!' Certainly, we are not all John Wesleys – but the point he is making is a vital one for us all the same.

As we know from this passage and others, Jesus consistently carved out time from his busy ministry to be alone with God, deepening and strengthening his relationship with his heavenly Father. And if Jesus needed this time, how much more do we? And yet we often find this difficult. Delia Smith once said that, the moment she decided to have some quiet time with God, a million 'urgent' things would flood into her mind which just had to be done *now*. I can certainly identify with that!

We know that human relationships need committed time together if they are to prosper, and our relationship with God is no different. Often, important decisions followed Jesus' times of prayer, such as here, with his choosing of the twelve apostles. When we lay ourselves, our questions, and our problems before God in prayer, we will probably not get immediate answers, but we may find our over-busy minds calmed, our perspective sharpened, and a sense, however faint, that there is a 'still, small voice' at the centre of our being. We are not walking alone.

Lord God, in our over-busy, distracted lives, help us seek your quiet presence, with a longing to grow in our relationship with you, our loving heavenly Father. Amen.

BARBARA MOSSE

Glory revealed

Jesus took with him Peter and John and James and went up on the mountain to pray. And while he was praying, the appearance of his face changed, and his clothes became as bright as a flash of lightning. Suddenly they saw two men, Moses and Elijah, talking to him... Now Peter and his companions... saw his glory... Peter said to Jesus, 'Master, it is good for us to be here; let us set up three tents...' not realising what he was saying. While he was saying this, a cloud came and overshadowed them, and they were terrified... Then from the cloud came a voice that said, 'This is my Son, my Chosen; listen to him!' When the voice had spoken, Jesus was found alone. And they kept silent and in those days told no one any of the things they had seen.

There was nothing unusual in Jesus going up a mountain to pray. Often he was alone, but on occasion, as here, he would take his inner core of three disciples with him. To begin with, the disciples fell asleep, as they would do again at another time of high tension and emotion, in the garden of Gethsemane (see Wednesday, 5 August). But when they were fully awake, what they saw was too much to make real sense of: a momentary glimpse of the glory beyond the veil, as Moses and Elijah speak with Jesus about the cross which lies ahead of him (v. 31).

We can perhaps identify with Peter in his wish to make this glory visible and permanent, but that cannot be; they must go back down the mountain and re-enter the struggle, pain, and suffering of ordinary life. The reality check comes when the cloud descends and the voice of God speaks directly to the disciples: 'This is my Son... listen to him!' (v. 35). Ordinary life must resume, and the disciples' continuing closeness to Jesus is vital.

The silence of the disciples may seem strange; in the other gospels it is Jesus who orders them not to speak. But Jesus knows that the crowds who came to him wouldn't yet be able to cope with such a revelation. Even Peter, James, and John struggled.

Lord Jesus Christ, open our ears we pray, that we may listen to you,
and our eyes that we may catch glimpses of your glory
in the midst of our daily lives. Amen.

BARBARA MOSSE

The heavenly Jerusalem

Therefore, since we are surrounded by so great a cloud of witnesses... let us run with perseverance the race that is set before us... Pursue peace with everyone and the holiness without which no one will see the Lord... You have not come to something that can be touched, a blazing fire, and darkness, and gloom, and a tempest, and the sound of a trumpet, and a voice whose words made the hearers beg that not another word be spoken to them... But you have come to Mount Zion and to the city of the living God, the heavenly Jerusalem, and to innumerable angels in festal gathering, and to the assembly of the firstborn who are enrolled in heaven, and to God the judge of all, and to the spirits of the righteous made perfect, and to Jesus the mediator of the new covenant.

Today's passage from Hebrews points towards the climax of our journey, a journey which properly began with Moses' encounter with God on Mount Sinai, and will become complete at Mount Zion and the heavenly Jerusalem. Like the original believers, we are still on that journey, but we feel that we are coming closer – almost within sight.

Here we see great hope and encouragement. The text employs the rhetorical device of vivid contrast to express its message; this is effective, but we do need to be careful. Some critics have used this contrast to demonstrate the triumph of Christianity over the Israelite religion. But we cannot reduce the message of this text in this way, not least because it provides a triumphant climax to the previous chapter, where an inspiring list of the Israelite heroes of faith are listed. They are the 'cloud of witnesses' mentioned at the beginning of our text, whose examples we are encouraged to follow.

A both/and approach rather than an either/or is more helpful. We need the closeness and intimacy with God that we have in Christ, without losing the sense of awe, wonder, and majesty expressed in the Mount Sinai theophany. Our God must always be a God who is beyond our human attempts to confine and domesticate.

Holy and awesome God, each day you surprise us afresh with the wonder and beauty of your presence. Help us to see the glory that surrounds us, and to worship you in gratitude and awe. Amen.

BARBARA MOSSE

Exodus 1—4

Moses is perhaps the most esteemed character in the Hebrew scriptures. He is the bringer of God's law, famously carved by God's own hand onto the two stone tablets which Moses then brings down from the mountain. These remain central to Christian worship today, as the ten commandments. Moses is also the one who leads the Israelites out of slavery in Egypt towards freedom in the promised land, the territory promised by God to Abraham centuries before. But all that is for later. Over these two weeks, we explore the start of the story, the events which led up to Moses assuming leadership of his people.

I trust that, in doing so, we will develop a greater familiarity with that period in Israel's history. But I hope we will also find that a text written long before the time of Jesus can give us fresh insights into how we face some of the challenges and opportunities of life today. For me, this is always one of the most exciting aspects of scripture. Because it brings fresh perspective, while being deeply embedded in the relationship between humanity and God, it is doubly precious.

Exodus was not written at the time of the events it depicts. The oral traditions it drew on probably reached written form at least 500 years later than when these events are said to have taken place. Like most of the oldest parts of the Hebrew scriptures, it was always intended to be more a work of theological reflection than a direct historical record. That is not, however, to undermine or deny the deep truths that it conveys as, over its 40 chapters, it describes how the covenant between God and his chosen people takes a critical step forward.

The story of Moses has, right up to the present day, provided an inspiration to oppressed peoples seeking hope for liberation. It lies behind the words of many of the spirituals sung by people of African descent who were enslaved in the Caribbean and North America. Its story was felt to be so seditious that Exodus was almost entirely excluded from a special version of the Bible printed in 1807 for use by enslaved workers in the British West Indies.

DAVID WALKER

An oppressed minority

Therefore they set taskmasters over them to oppress them with forced labour. They built supply cities, Pithom and Rameses, for Pharaoh. But the more they were oppressed, the more they multiplied and spread, so that the Egyptians came to dread the Israelites. The Egyptians subjected the Israelites to hard servitude and made their lives bitter with hard servitude in mortar and bricks and in every kind of field labour. They were ruthless in all the tasks that they imposed on them.

Pharaoh and his court are concerned that the Hebrew minority, who had been invited to settle in Egypt back in the time of Joseph, cannot be trusted to be loyal to his regime. Their fears are increased by the fact that the Hebrew community is growing as a proportion of the population. Hence, they respond by seeking to make life as harsh and unpleasant as they can.

If that sounds familiar, I am not surprised. Fear of migrant minorities, especially those of other faiths, and with higher birth rates than the host population, is as prevalent today as in Moses' time. We hear it in the rhetoric of politicians, including in Europe and America. In recent years such voices have only gained in strength. Yet the Hebrews in Egypt, like the vast majority of migrant communities across the globe today, simply wanted to live their lives in peace and to practise their faith.

Antisemitism, in particular, seems to be on the rise again, aided by the fact that few of us remain from the generations who lived through the fascist atrocities of the mid-20th century. My home in Salford is in an area with one of the highest concentrations of Jewish population in the UK. It grieves me to see the security measures that need to be in place to allow local people to access their places of worship and for their children to get to and from school in safety.

Heavenly Father, we pray for all who live as minorities, especially those subject to prejudice or oppression. Turn the hearts of both leaders of the nations, and the populations they serve, away from the fear of those of other faiths and backgrounds, that your children may live in increasing harmony and hospitality. Amen.

DAVID WALKER

Civil disobedience

The king of Egypt said to the Hebrew midwives, one of whom was named Shiphrah and the other Puah, 'When you act as midwives to the Hebrew women and see them on the birthstool, if it is a son, kill him; but if it is a daughter, she shall live.' But the midwives feared God; they did not do as the king of Egypt commanded them, but they let the boys live… Then Pharaoh commanded all his people, 'Every son that is born to the Hebrews you shall throw into the Nile, but you shall let every daughter live.'

Harsh working conditions have failed to halt the growth of the Hebrew population in Egypt, so Pharaoh turns to more drastic measures. Male children represent the main threat as, once grown up, they could assist an invader against his own forces. The midwives now tasked with committing this act of genocide are caught in a dilemma. How should they respond when the law of the land commands them to do something they are convinced is opposed to the will of God?

In the end, the midwives found an excuse which forced Pharaoh to turn to others to do his bidding. They escaped with their lives. But the moral of the story is that their obedience to God outweighed their obedience to the king.

There is a long and honourable tradition of peaceful civil disobedience by Christians. We see it in the underground churches operating in countries where acts of worship are strictly controlled or even banned. It also happens in Britain. Some Christians have chosen to break the law to make a strong and visible protest against what they see as a failure by government to address the climate emergency. One may not agree with their cause or the means by which they prosecute it, one may even think it counterproductive, but I recognise that they are motivated by a moral issue as pressing for them as was the challenge the Hebrew midwives faced in Egypt.

Lord God, we hold before you all those who feel their choice lies between following human authorities and obedience to your will. Grant them strength to know when to hold firm, and wisdom to understand when to yield. For Jesus' sake. Amen.

DAVID WALKER

Two women of faith

Then his sister said to Pharaoh's daughter, 'Shall I go and get you a nurse from the Hebrew women to nurse the child for you?' Pharaoh's daughter said to her, 'Yes.' So the girl went and called the child's mother. Pharaoh's daughter said to her, 'Take this child and nurse it for me, and I will give you your wages.' So the woman took the child and nursed it. When the child grew up, she brought him to Pharaoh's daughter, and he became her son.

I do love this little episode. Moses' mother obeyed the law by putting her infant son into the river; however, the waterproofed basket allows him to live long enough for Pharaoh's daughter to rescue the child. Furthermore, the cunning plan results in his being returned to his mother to nurse and bring up, while she even gets paid a wage for doing so. I have sometimes referred to this story as the earliest recorded example of child benefit payment!

As with many stories in the scriptures, we are not told directly what part God has actually played. What we read is a tale of how two Hebrew women devise a plan that will draw a third person, one in a position of real power, into saving the child. Their understanding of how another woman will react on finding a vulnerable, three-month-old baby in a basket turns out to be accurate. And they do all this without any awareness that this child has a special destiny.

I see the hand of God not in a miracle, but in the faith in him that the two women have. A significant portion of the Hebrew scriptures is often referred to as the Wisdom Books. Being attuned to God through this tradition remains a hallmark of how his followers are called to live their lives today, just as much as in biblical times. We too are invited to immerse ourselves in that same godly wisdom which will sometimes, as it did for Moses' mother and sister, lead us in unexpected directions.

Lord God, grant each of us such wisdom as is needful for us to do your will here on earth and so further your kingdom. Amen.

DAVID WALKER

Executing justice

One day after Moses had grown up, he went out to his people and saw their forced labour. He saw an Egyptian beating a Hebrew, one of his own people. He looked this way and that, and seeing no one he killed the Egyptian and hid him in the sand. When he went out the next day, he saw two Hebrews fighting, and he said to the one who was in the wrong, 'Why do you strike your fellow Hebrew?' He answered, 'Who made you a ruler and judge over us? Do you mean to kill me as you killed the Egyptian?'

Moses will become the one to whom God gives the basics of the law, the ten commandments, inscribed on tablets of stone, and who then seeks to adjudicate it for the rest of his life. However, his first attempts at judgement, many years earlier, prove clumsy and ineffectual. As a consequence, he has to flee for his life; he will not return to Egypt for several decades. When he does return, he will have a direct answer to the question with which his fellow Hebrew challenges him. Moses will indeed have been made 'ruler and judge' over the people, not by Pharaoh, nor by some process of appointment within the Hebrew community, but by God.

Along the way he will learn important lessons, including that the penalty meted out for an offence must never be greater than the crime. The phrase 'an eye for an eye, a tooth for a tooth', which remains well known even today, may sound brutal, but it is about limiting punishment, avoiding the escalation of wrongdoing. I have found myself quoting it on occasion in Parliament, when a penalty is proposed that seems excessive to the original harm done.

Moreover, Moses will recognise that justice needs to follow a proper process. It cannot be the peremptory action he takes here. In years to come, he will set up a full legal system, appointing others as judges to hear less complex cases, so that his time and energy can be concentrated where it is most needed.

Heavenly Father, may the systems of justice in our own country and generation reflect the sound principles first established by your servant Moses. Amen.

DAVID WALKER

Supporting the weak

Moses fled from Pharaoh. He settled in the land of Midian and sat down by a well. The priest of Midian had seven daughters. They came to draw water and filled the troughs to water their father's flock. But some shepherds came and drove them away. Moses got up and came to their defence and watered their flock. When they returned to their father Reuel, he said, 'How is it that you have come back so soon today?' They said, 'An Egyptian helped us against the shepherds; he even drew water for us and watered the flock.'

From the shepherds' perspective, might is right. They have the power to drive away the women who have already done the hard work of drawing water from the well and then take the fruits of those labours for themselves. Why should they wait until the women have watered their own animals? Why should they bother to draw water themselves when they can take possession of what is already there?

In taking the side of the women, Moses establishes an important principle of justice: that it should seek to redress the inevitable imbalance between the powerful and the weak. All will be treated as equal under the law. In future generations, this will come to be central to the nature of kingship and of all in public office in Israel, and be passed down as a cornerstone in our own legal traditions today. International human rights law rests on the Judeo-Christian foundations which Moses is building here.

Sadly, while long usage may make these principles seem self-evident, they remain often discarded or ignored. Autocratic leaders exploit their people, while the super-wealthy use their resources to get laws changed or to bend their application in their favour. Across the globe, we see nations invade, colonise, or seek to annex weaker neighbours, especially those whose natural resources, including water, precious minerals, and agricultural fertility, they want to appropriate.

Lord God, look with mercy on those who are oppressed by the strong and powerful. As Moses helped the women at the well, may we be your advocates in seeking and obtaining justice for both individuals and nations today. Amen.

DAVID WALKER

The burning bush

Moses said, 'I must turn aside and look at this great sight and see why the bush is not burned up.' When the Lord saw that he had turned aside to see, God called to him out of the bush, 'Moses, Moses!' And he said, 'Here I am.' Then he said, 'Come no closer! Remove the sandals from your feet, for the place on which you are standing is holy ground.' He said further, 'I am the God of your father, the God of Abraham, the God of Isaac, and the God of Jacob.' And Moses hid his face, for he was afraid to look at God.

Fires in open country are common enough; hot and dry conditions create an ideal context for combustion. What surprises Moses, and makes him turn aside on his travels, is the fact that the bush at the centre of the blaze seems unaffected by the flames. His attentiveness in noticing raises his curiosity. He stops to take a closer look, and there, amid the conflagration, he meets God.

Rowan Williams, in his years as Archbishop of Canterbury, used to describe the task of the church as being very simple – to notice what God is up to and join in. Sadly, very often, both as individuals and church communities, we are so busy getting on with the tasks and demands of life, pursuing our own plans, that we either fail to notice the presence and action of God among us or we are too preoccupied to pause and pay attention to it.

There are times when, in visiting a parish, I will reflect to the congregation where I think I have spotted God at work among them. It may be their ministry with a particular group within their membership or their neighbours. It may be that God has begun adding to their numbers people from a different age group, ethnicity, or social background. Sometimes, an outsider can point out what is so close to us that we have failed to see it.

Heavenly Father, we thank you that Moses saw, stopped, and turned aside at the burning bush. Help us also to recognise the signs of your presence and work among us, and to join in. Amen.

DAVID WALKER

Disputed territory

The Lord said, 'I have observed the misery of my people who are in Egypt; I have heard their cry on account of their taskmasters. Indeed, I know their sufferings, and I have come down to deliver them from the Egyptians and to bring them up out of that land to a good and spacious land, to a land flowing with milk and honey, to the country of the Canaanites, the Hittites, the Amorites, the Perizzites, the Hivites, and the Jebusites.'

Back in the days of Joseph, the Hebrews arrived in Egypt as migrants, escaping the drought and famine that had engulfed their former lands. Generations have passed, and while Egypt has never truly felt like home, long familiarity has blunted any pressing desire to reclaim the land God promised to Abraham. It is only now, when their hosts have turned hostile, that a move becomes imperative. However, Canaan has once again become a land 'flowing with milk and honey', and other peoples have settled it. They are unlikely to view a huge influx of Abraham's descendants, claiming ownership, in a positive light.

Territorial claims and counterclaims remain as present and pressing a factor today as in the time of Moses, not least in the Holy Lands. There are the Jewish communities who, in the aftermath of World War II, saw themselves as returning to their ancestral lands, where they would never again be subject to the genocide of the Holocaust. On the other side are the Palestinians who had been the majority population for many generations. Elsewhere, Russia claimed Ukraine was part of historic Holy Rus, and in Africa boundaries set by the European colonial powers at the Berlin Conference of the 1880s continue to cause conflict.

There are rarely easy solutions; most people prefer to live in an independent nation, large enough to be secure against threat, and in which those like themselves form a dominant majority, yet too often one group's safe majority status confines another to minority and subjection.

Lord Jesus, we may not be able to resolve the many disputes over land and inheritance that scar your creation. But, wherever we can, let us be agents for peaceful living together. Amen.

DAVID WALKER

What's in a name?

But Moses said to God, 'If I come to the Israelites and say to them, "The God of your ancestors has sent me to you," and they ask me, "What is his name?" what shall I say to them?' God said to Moses, 'I AM WHO I AM.' He said further, 'Thus you shall say to the Israelites, "I AM has sent me to you."' God also said to Moses, 'Thus you shall say to the Israelites, "The Lord, the God of your ancestors, the God of Abraham, the God of Isaac, and the God of Jacob, has sent me to you."'

I discovered, on my first day at school, that there were three of us called David in my class. My dad, who I suspect had chosen my name, suggested that it might help everyone if I let myself be known by my middle name. I was not having that. David was how I had always thought of myself; to suddenly become Stuart would confuse my sense of who I was.

Names matter. In biblical and other cultures they often carry specific meanings and define a person's role or destiny. Meanwhile, to know someone's true name can be seen as a powerful factor in gaining influence over them, so much so that hidden and secret names are not uncommon. Here in this passage, God gives his name to Moses. In older Bibles it was often written in English as Jehovah, though modern scholarship suggests a more likely pronunciation would have been Yahweh. That uncertainty arises in part because the name of God was so sacred that it became forbidden in Judaism to speak it aloud.

So Moses' request to be able to tell the Israelites God's name makes good sense. Yet the answer he gets is intriguing. 'I am who I am,' says God. 'Tell them, "I am" has sent me to you.' Putting it bluntly, God is making clear that he cannot be constrained or limited by any specific name, nor can anyone gain power over him by knowing his name. He will be just who and what he chooses to be, sovereign and independent of human control.

Heavenly Father, may we never seek to limit or control you,
but be ever ready to do your will. Amen.

DAVID WALKER

A promise of freedom

'They will listen to your voice, and you and the elders of Israel shall go to the king of Egypt and say to him, "The Lord, the God of the Hebrews, has met with us; let us now go a three days' journey into the wilderness, so that we may sacrifice to the Lord our God." I know, however, that the king of Egypt will not let you go except by a mighty hand. So I will stretch out my hand and strike Egypt with all my wonders that I will perform in it; after that he will let you go.'

At a first glance, the request with which Moses and the elders are to go to Pharaoh is a modest one: simply to be allowed to go and worship. It would take them away from their labours for little more than a week. God knows, however, that the king cannot accede to it. Pharaoh has no guarantee that they will return and, even if they did, their time away would have emboldened them. It flies in the face of his policy of using ever-harsher treatment to keep the Israelites demoralised and subdued. There is no stable halfway point between slavery and freedom.

Recently, researching the Church of England's entanglement with the transatlantic slave trade, I came across a book known as the Slave Bible. Printed in 1807, for the use of enslaved workers on plantations in the British West Indies, it excised all passages that might lead the readers to believe they should be emancipated. This entire book of Exodus, so central to Jewish identity and the source of much Christian theology, was reduced to little more than the ten commandments. Indeed, as they began to gain biblical knowledge from other sources, these were the stories, often turned into spiritual songs, that inspired the enslaved in their struggle to gain their freedom.

Even today, slavery, often couched in more modern forms, remains a stain on humanity. And Christian campaigners continue to draw on the story of Moses and the Exodus, to ground and inspire their efforts.

Great God, you set your people free. Help us to work for the liberation of all who remain enslaved today. Amen.

DAVID WALKER

A lack of confidence

But Moses said to the Lord, 'O my Lord, I have never been eloquent, neither in the past nor even now that you have spoken to your servant, but I am slow of speech and slow of tongue.' Then the Lord said to him, 'Who gives speech to mortals? Who makes them mute or deaf, seeing or blind? Is it not I, the Lord? Now go, and I will be with your mouth and teach you what you are to speak.' But he said, 'O my Lord, please send someone else.'

I hardly dare think how often, in the face of some unenviable duty, I must have echoed those words from the end of our Bible reading. Moses comes up with all the objections as to why his inadequacies mean he is not the best candidate for the job. How can someone who is not a natural public speaker possibly be the one to lead the Israelites to freedom? God's answer is pretty blunt. He is one who gives humans the power of speech; is Moses now doubting that God can and will give him the appropriate words to utter at the right moment?

I love my work as a bishop, but there are times when I know that what I have to do lies beyond the gifts I am confident in exercising. Yet, again and again, if I am able to get beyond that initial echoing of Moses' words, I discover that God is more than able to make up the difference.

There is one proviso, though. As the old saying goes, 'God helps those who help themselves.' God expects me to do my best. Often my most challenging tasks involve meetings where different voices, with conflicting hopes, need to be brought to a conclusion all will accept. If I go into such an encounter underprepared, trusting God to do all the heavy lifting, I am going to be disappointed. It is when I have prepared properly and prayed about the matter that I can be confident God will work with me to bridge the gap. After that, if the problem remains intractable, I can leave it in God's hands.

Lord, when my own abilities fall short, be my strength,
my aid, my wisdom, that your will be done. Amen.

DAVID WALKER

Working in partnership

Then the anger of the Lord was kindled against Moses, and he said, 'What of your brother Aaron, the Levite? I know that he can speak well; even now he is coming out to meet you, and when he sees you his heart will be glad. You shall speak to him and put the words in his mouth, and I will be with your mouth and with his mouth and will teach you what you shall do. He indeed shall speak for you to the people; he shall serve as a mouth for you, and you shall serve as God for him.'

Despite God's reassurances, Moses remains adamant that his speaking skills are not up to the task. I love this passage, because it makes clear that God has a Plan B. If Moses will not speak, then his brother Aaron, who is a naturally gifted speaker, will. Yet rather than Moses being replaced by Aaron, the two brothers will work in future as a partnership: Aaron will speak with the Israelites, Moses will speak with God. Up to this point, the story of God's people has been very much focused on individual leaders, such as Abraham, Isaac, Jacob, and Joseph, each of whom has had the full range of skills for leadership.

I find a double comfort in this. First, that God is flexible in achieving his purposes. It may be that my sins and failings close one door, but God will always have another door he can open. However badly I mess up, even if I resist God directly, I cannot thwart God's ultimate purposes.

Second, much of what God asks me to do, he does not require me to do alone. Pretty well all my adult life I have been blessed by being surrounded by others who complement my gifts. Indeed, I have learned to try to ensure I am always working as part of a diverse team, rather than with those who look and think and act like me. They will spot things I have not seen, and bring insights and perspectives that would never have occurred to me.

Lord, help me to work with others, especially those different from myself, that together we may fulfil your plans. Amen.

DAVID WALKER

Symbols of authority

Moses went back to his father-in-law Jethro and said to him, 'Please let me go back to my own people in Egypt and see whether they are still living.' And Jethro said to Moses, 'Go in peace.' The Lord said to Moses in Midian, 'Go back to Egypt, for all those who were seeking your life are dead.' So Moses took his wife and his sons, put them on a donkey, and went back to the land of Egypt, and Moses carried the staff of God in his hand.

Much of the UK population, along with viewers from around the globe, watched King Charles III's coronation service in May 2023. The ceremonies provided a riot of colour and ritual. At various times, particular symbolic objects, such as the sword carried by a cabinet minister and the crown itself, played a prominent part. Symbolic objects matter. For me, the cross around my neck and the shepherd's crook I carry represent the authority and responsibility I bear as a bishop, while also reminding me and others of the Christ to whom I am accountable.

Beyond the church, whenever I enter the House of Lords, I bow to the cloth of state behind the throne. Meanwhile, each day's proceedings begin with the Lord Speaker's procession, which is led by an official carrying the ornate mace. The mace must be in its place on the woolsack, another ritual object, whenever the House is sitting. These objects symbolise both the authority of the House and that it exists to serve the Crown.

In today's scripture passage, Moses carries his own symbol of authority, the staff of God. With it, he will later perform miracles. But this is no mere magic wand, such as the magicians of the Egyptian court might have carried. Such magical devices point purely to themselves or to the one who holds them, not to a greater power behind them. Nor do they indicate any sense of accountability on behalf of the bearer. Moses' staff, like the symbolic objects in church and state, are all ultimately pointers to God, the one from whom all power and authority flows and to whom all are accountable.

Lord, help me to live each day exercising such responsibility as you have given me, yet always in your faithful service. Amen.

DAVID WALKER

A difficult story

And the Lord said to Moses, 'When you go back to Egypt, see that you perform before Pharaoh all the wonders that I have put in your power, but I will harden his heart, so that he will not let the people go. Then you shall say to Pharaoh, "Thus says the Lord: Israel is my firstborn son. I said to you, 'Let my son go that he may serve me.' But you refused to let him go; now I will kill your firstborn son."'

I find this a tricky passage. Its plain sense is that God will deliberately act to prevent Pharaoh from granting Moses' request, but will then kill the king's firstborn son as punishment. Later chapters will list the numerous times Moses pleads with Pharaoh and the succession of plagues that eventually lead, on the night of the Exodus, not only to the death of Pharaoh's firstborn, but that of every family in Egypt apart from the Israelites. God's treatment of Pharaoh seems a long way from the loving Father of whom Jesus teaches, so much so that some early Christians speculated that these must be different gods.

I do not go along with that. Jesus is clear that his Father is the God of Abraham and Moses. But what I do recognise is that I need to interpret particular passages of scripture in the light of the overarching themes of the Bible. There has long been a tradition in some Bible versions of printing the words of Jesus in red, so that they stand out as deserving extra special attention and carrying particular authority. I like how this helps emphasise that he is the lens through which we should look at all scripture.

I know too that there are places where one Bible verse directly contradicts another, even on such crucial points as the timing of the crucifixion. Like many Christians, I believe the scriptures are divinely inspired, not divinely dictated. They were written down by faithful followers of God but, as in this case, often many years later. Ultimately, I do not believe God deliberately orchestrated the mass murder of Egyptian boys.

Lord Jesus, help me when reading scripture, to see it always through the lens of your life and teaching. Amen.

DAVID WALKER

Proof of God's purposes and intent

Moses told Aaron all the words of the Lord with which he had sent him and all the signs with which he had charged him. Then Moses and Aaron went and assembled all the elders of the Israelites. Aaron spoke all the words that the Lord had spoken to Moses and performed the signs in the sight of the people. The people believed, and when they heard that the Lord had given heed to the Israelites and that he had seen their misery, they bowed down and worshipped.

What Moses is explaining to the Israelites is huge. After several centuries of increasingly harsh conditions in Egypt, God is planning to take them back to their former home, in the land long promised to Abraham and his descendants. Egypt might be tough, but it is familiar. Seeking to escape may well bring down the wrath of Pharaoh on them, with dire consequences. Who is this God? Can he really enable a bunch of runaway slaves to defeat Pharaoh's well-equipped military, with all its horses and chariots? In response, the signs that Moses performs are convincing. They prove not only that God has the strength to accomplish the task, but also that he sees their plight and will fight on their side.

The old proverb 'Seeing is believing' holds much truth. St Thomas famously would not accept that Jesus was risen from the dead unless he could both see and touch him. He knew that if it were true, it would be life-changing. It is a common, and entirely proper, human trait that the more impact something will have on us, the higher the level of proof we require before making a commitment. The candidates I ordain as deacons and priests have to affirm that they are convinced of their calling. More commonly, the introduction to the wedding service reminds the couple that marriage should not be undertaken lightly, but only after careful thought. Like the Israelites, we seek confirmation of God's will ahead of our commitment. Like them, once we have that assurance, it is then time to act.

Lord, when I am faced with a difficult task, help me to know your will
and be assured of your strength and power behind me,
and to act accordingly. Amen.

DAVID WALKER

Amos

Biblical prophets do not hold back their verbal punches, and in this respect, Amos is one of the best. Little is known about Amos himself apart from what is revealed in this book. We know he was from Tekoa, a town near the border between the north and the south kingdoms of Israel. We also hear that he was not a prophet by descent or profession, as some were, but rather was a herdsman and a 'dresser of sycamore trees' (7:14, NRSV), an odd term that is likely to mean he tended the fruit of sycamore-fig trees to make sure they ripened.

The context was that for the first time in generations the nation of Israel was in a period of peace and prosperity. It had been about 150 years since the conflict that divided the two kingdoms – Israel to the north and Judah to the south – and their people were enjoying the benefits of peace. The trouble is they were enjoying them rather too much and had become complacent, turned away from God, and were mistreating those who were poor and vulnerable.

We do not hear much of what happened when Amos received God's call to leave his land and work; all we know is that 'the Lord took me from tending the flock and said to me, "Go, prophesy to my people Israel"' (7:15, NIV). Amos responds with obedience.

The book of Amos is a compilation of messages and visions broadly structured into three main sections. Chapters 1—2 are a series of judgements made against the nations surrounding Israel and then Israel itself; chapters 3—6 are a series of sermons directed towards Israel; and chapters 7—9 are five prophetic visions which describe the coming judgement.

What is striking is the literary skill Amos displays in his use of poetry, repetition, visual imagery, and attention-grabbing turns of phrase, such as 'Hear this word, you cows of Bashan' (4:1). He may have been a rural farmer, but he was certainly highly skilled and well educated.

Amos is not an easy read, but the main themes are relevant to us today. God cares about how we treat one another, being people of God comes with both promise and challenge, and external signs of religiosity are nothing without social justice.

CLARE HAYNS

The Lord roars

The words of Amos, one of the shepherds of Tekoa – the vision he saw concerning Israel two years before the earthquake, when Uzziah was king of Judah and Jeroboam son of Jehoash was king of Israel. He said: 'The Lord roars from Zion and thunders from Jerusalem; the pastures of the shepherds dry up, and the top of Carmel withers.'

Amos begins with a prelude which sets the scene and establishes the tone for the rest of the book. I recently watched a youth workshop led by the percussion section of a world-class orchestra. At the end the children were let loose on the drums and cymbals, and it was, as you can imagine, incredibly loud! This is how the book of Amos begins – loudly, with a bang and a clash.

We are told that Amos hears God's call at a time when the kings were Uzziah of Judah (783–742 BCE) and Jeroboam II of Israel (786–746 BCE). The earthquake referred to was likely to be the one in around 760 BCE in northern Galilee, which was remembered two centuries later in Zechariah 14:5.

Here, Amos is bringing a message of judgement from the Lord, who 'roars' and 'thunders' (v. 2). Why is the Lord so angry, and who is this anger directed at? In this section, God's wrath is focused on the seven neighbours of Israel. They had been violent towards Israel and others (v. 3), were engaged in slavery (v. 6), had broken treaties with Israel (v. 9), and had treated women horrifically (v. 11). Amos' message was clear: God knows and sees what they are doing and there will be judgement; unjust kings would be exiled (v. 5), and their cities would be destroyed (v. 14).

It is as if Amos was sent with a loud cymbal to wake them up. Human beings, made in the image of God, should not treat one another like this. He is remarkably brave. It is one thing to notice injustice happening around us, but quite another to speak up about it.

Give us, O God, the courage to speak up when we see injustice and the faith to trust that you are with us when we do. Amen.

CLARE HAYNS

Remember who you are

This is what the Lord says: 'For three sins of Israel, even for four, I will not relent. They sell the innocent for silver, and the needy for a pair of sandals. They trample on the heads of the poor as on the dust of the ground and deny justice to the oppressed… I brought you up out of Egypt and led you forty years in the wilderness.'

Chapter 2 begins with Amos outlining a series of God's judgements which will be laid upon Israel's near neighbours. We might imagine the nation of Israel enjoying these declarations! Each prophesy follows the same pattern as in the chapter before – the statement 'For three sins… even for four', then a list of their sins, followed by a description of what the punishment was to be. Most of the sins of the neighbouring nations were to do with atrocities committed in war – taking slaves, razing cities, killing women and children.

But if there was any sense of schadenfreude (taking delight in the suffering of others), that ended abruptly here. Amos now turns his attention to the northern kingdom of Israel with a judgement that is the longest and most detailed. This begins a series of passages where God reminds Israel who they are, who their God is, and how far they have strayed from the covenant relationship made with Abraham.

God is a God of justice and righteousness and, in contrast, the Israelites had been treating one another with contempt and had used their 'religion' to condone all kinds of immoral behaviours. They had denied justice to those who needed it, had misused sacred places, and had even been taking wine as fines and then drinking it in the temple (vv. 6–8). Under covenant law, no Hebrew person could be kept as a slave against their will (Deuteronomy 15:1–18), and yet here people were being sold 'for a pair of sandals'. The Lord is not impressed, to say the least.

Through Amos, God reminds them of where they have come from. They were rescued from slavery themselves once: 'I brought you up out of Egypt' (v. 10). There is a sense of disappointment – the Lord expected better from them.

Thank you, Lord, that even when we stray from your will, you guide us back to you. Amen.

CLARE HAYNS

The lion roars

Does a lion roar in the thicket when it has no prey?... When a trumpet sounds in a city, do not the people tremble?… Surely the Sovereign Lord does nothing without revealing his plan to his servants the prophets. The lion has roared – who will not fear? The Sovereign Lord has spoken – who can but prophesy?

Have you ever heard a lion roaring in the wild? I have once, on a safari trip in Zimbabwe, and I will never forget it. Thankfully it was quite far away, and we were on a boat, but it was a sound that made the hairs on the back of my neck stand up.

Amos began with the voice of God like the roaring of a lion, and here the lion is roaring once again, but this time it is Amos who is responding. No one could expect to make the dire predictions that Amos was making without facing some opposition. Amos 3—5 consists of three sermons against Israel, all beginning the same way: 'Hear this word.' Here, in the first of these sermons, Amos justifies why he is speaking out as he is.

The chapter begins with a series of rhetorical questions: 'Does a lion roar in the thicket when it has no prey?' (v. 4); 'Does a trap spring up… if it has not caught anything?' (v. 5); 'When a trumpet sounds in a city, do not the people tremble?' (v. 6). These are all leading up to the most important question. If the Lord had called him to speak up, then could he do anything other than respond (v. 8)?

The answer was, of course, no. Amos would have to speak up. The lion was roaring, and he trembled; the Lord was speaking, and he had to convey the message, even though it was hard to hear.

There are times when we need to stand up for what we know is right, even when that comes at a cost.

Lord, give us the courage to respond to your call. Amen.

CLARE HAYNS

'You cows of Bashan'

Hear this word, you cows of Bashan on Mount Samaria, you women who oppress the poor and crush the needy… 'Go to Bethel and sin; go to Gilgal and sin yet more. Bring your sacrifices every morning, your tithes every three years. Burn leavened bread as a thank offering and brag about your freewill offerings – boast about them, you Israelites, for this is what you love to do,' declares the Sovereign Lord.

There is not much light within the darkness as the prophet continues his sermon setting out all the sins of the people of Israel. The chapter begins with Amos comparing the wives of Israel's leaders to the fat, well-fed cows of Mount Samaria, an insult that would have been as offensive then as it would be today. Amos goes on to name all the ways God had tried to get the attention of his people over the years, through famine, drought, ruined crops, plagues, and even death in battle (vv. 6–11). Each attempt had failed and the plaintive cry 'Yet you have not returned to me' is repeated five times.

The passage above is ironic. When Amos says, 'Go to Bethel and sin,' he is not suggesting this is what the people should do! Both Bethel and Gilgal were important religious shrines, and their priests would have instructed the people to go there. The main complaint in this section is not that the people had been ignoring the obligations of their faith. They had been bringing sacrifices, tithing, burning thank offerings – all right acts according to their law. The problem was that despite all these external signs of religion, they had not returned to God. The Israelites were so focused on wanting to look good in the eyes of others that they had ignored the poor and those in need.

Jesus issued a similar warning when he accused the Pharisees of being 'whitewashed tombs' (Matthew 23:27). It is a reminder that God is not interested in outward signs of faith if these are not matched in how we act towards others.

Lord, forgive us when we worship you with our lips
but not our actions. Amen.

CLARE HAYNS

Let justice roll on

Seek good, not evil, that you may live. Then the Lord God Almighty will be with you, just as you say he is. Hate evil, love good; maintain justice in the courts. Perhaps the Lord God Almighty will have mercy on the remnant of Joseph… But let justice roll on like a river, righteousness like a never-failing stream!

On 28 August 1963, Martin Luther King Jr stood on the steps of the Lincoln Memorial in Washington, DC and quoted from the book of Amos in his famous 'I Have a Dream' speech. Steeped in the Bible, he drew on this book for imagery to call out a nation which was oppressing black people and denying them their rights through segregation and other unjust laws.

Having had several chapters lamenting Israel's sins, we now have a glimmer of hope. It begins with a plea for the people to turn away from ritualistic worship to 'seek the Lord and live' (v. 6). The call is to 'seek good, not evil' (v. 14) and to maintain 'justice in the courts' (v. 15). The word 'good' is often defined in Amos as justice in the courts, as opposed to 'evil', which is understood as judicial corruption and economic exploitation.

There are two conditional promises here to give hope. One is that if the people seek good, then 'the Lord God Almighty will be with you'. The other is that if they love good, then 'perhaps' God will have mercy on them. The rest of the chapter explores the important concept of the 'day of the Lord'. It was understood to be a time of victory for Israel, which the people looked forward to, but Amos warns them that it is also a time for justice (vv. 18–19).

Justice 'rolling like a river' is not the gentle trickle of a stream (or a wadi) which only flows after rainfall; it is the gushing flood of water which sweeps away all that is evil. The righteousness of God is not going to dry up; rather it is 'never failing'.

Seeking and loving God (good) may involve us speaking up for those who have been overlooked, and to do this we may have to get our feet wet!

Lord God, we pray for justice in our world. Amen.

CLARE HAYNS

Richer than yow!

Woe to you who are complacent in Zion, and to you who feel secure on Mount Samaria, you notable men of the foremost nation, to whom the people of Israel come! Go to Kalneh and look at it; go from there to great Hamath, and then go down to Gath in Philistia. Are they better off than your two kingdoms? Is their land larger than yours?

Stan and Pam Herbert were a hilariously awful couple in the sketch show *Harry Enfield and Chums*. They would look down their noses at their neighbours, boasting in a broad West Midlands accent about how they were 'considerably richer than yow'!

The prophet now shines a light on the people of the two capitals of the kingdoms, Zion and Samaria. They had fallen into the traps of complacency and superiority, common dangers of the spiritual life. Rather than being thankful for the time of security and prosperity, they had become complacent. They were 'notable men of the foremost nation' and as such were supposed to be showing a good example. But they had been doing the opposite, showing off their wealth and turning their backs on the poor.

The prophet points them to look towards notable cities, Kalneh and Hamath to the north and Gath to the west. These places had all once been prosperous, but had all suffered defeats in the previous century. What makes them think they would be any different?

Alongside this, the religious leaders had begun to think they were superior because they were chosen by God. Amos calls this out and reminds them that just because they were chosen, this does not mean they are in any way deserving of this or better than anyone else.

It is easy to slip into these traps. We can be complacent in our faith when things are going well and when we are not facing particular challenges. Like Stan and Pam Herbert, we can also look down our noses at those without faith or those with other faiths. Amos reminds us not to fall into these traps.

Help us, Lord, to be always thankful for your love and grace,
never forgetting you give more than we can ever deserve.

CLARE HAYNS

The Lord relented

This is what the Sovereign Lord showed me: he was preparing swarms of locusts after the king's share had been harvested and just as the late crops were coming up. When they had stripped the land clean, I cried out, 'Sovereign Lord, forgive! How can Jacob survive? He is so small!' So the Lord relented. 'This will not happen,' the Lord said.

What are we doing when we pray? Is it possible for mere humans to change God's mind? These are challenging questions. There are plenty of examples in the Bible of people crying out to God, and here we have an example of God seeming to change direction as a result.

The final section of Amos consists of five visions of the future of Israel. Here, Amos is shown a plague of locusts in the process of destroying the land. The reference to 'late crops' probably refers to the second crop which the people depended on to feed their families and livestock after the royal tax had been paid. This would be catastrophic, leading to destitution without any hope of help from the political leaders.

Amos is moved by what he sees, and he cries out to God, interceding on their behalf, for God to be compassionate and merciful. He seems to accept that the people deserve punishment, but his pleas are for forgiveness. His reasoning is that the land is small and the people vulnerable; they could not survive this. Amos' prayers are answered and the Lord 'relented' (the Hebrew term basically means 'changed'), and the plague was averted: 'This will not happen' (v. 3).

There may be situations in our world or lives that move us to cry out in prayer. We might wonder why we need to do this because surely God knows best, and all we can do is pray, 'Thy will be done.' This is a wonderful example of the dynamic relationship at the heart of God and humanity, where God's actions are changed because of a human's prayer. The future for the people was different because of Amos' pleas. Can our prayers make a difference? I think so.

Lord, thank you that you hear our prayers
and that they make a difference. Amen.

CLARE HAYNS

A basket of fruit

This is what the Sovereign Lord showed me: a basket of ripe fruit. 'What do you see, Amos?' he asked. 'A basket of ripe fruit,' I answered. Then the Lord said to me, 'The time is ripe for my people Israel; I will spare them no longer. In that day,' declares the Sovereign Lord, 'the songs in the temple will turn to wailing. Many, many bodies – flung everywhere! Silence!' Hear this, you who trample the needy and do away with the poor of the land.

It is perhaps no surprise that one of the visions given to Amos, the 'carer of fig trees', is that of a basket of ripe fruit. There is wordplay going on here which gets lost in translation. The Hebrew for 'ripe fruit' (*qayiṣ*) sounds very similar to 'the time is ripe'/'the end' (*qēṣ*).

This is the fourth of Amos' visions, the others so far being locusts, a fire, and a plumb-line (Amos 7). It is a simple, if bleak, message. A basket of ripe fruit signals the end of the summer season. This image drives home the lesson that the end of the season for repentance has come. God's patience has run out. The people had been given ample warnings and now, 'Silence!', it is decision time. Will they turn back to God and fulfil their covenant promises to love God and one another? Or will they carry on in their own selfish ways, oppressing the needy and turning their religious practice into idolatry?

The description of the coming judgement is stark. Worship songs will turn to cries, there will be death and destruction, and there will be a famine, not for food and water, but 'a famine of hearing the words of the Lord' (v. 11). It is the bleakest point in the entire book, even 'the sun [will] go down at noon and darken the earth in broad daylight' (v. 9).

Hundreds of years later this would happen when Jesus hung on the cross, where from 'noon until three in the afternoon darkness came over all the land' (Matthew 27:45).

Lord, be with us in times of darkness,
and give us hope in times of despair. Amen.

CLARE HAYNS

Restore and rebuild

'In that day I will restore David's fallen shelter – I will repair its broken wall and restore its ruins – and will rebuild it as it used to be, so that they may possess the remnant of Edom and all the nations that bear my name,' declares the Lord, who will do these things. 'The days are coming,' declares the Lord.

What a relief! This follows after the fifth apocalyptic vision, where Amos describes the Lord bringing about the destruction of a temple, which falls 'on the heads of all the people' (v. 1), and the death and exile of all Israel. It was to be a disaster, and yet even though they are told, 'I will destroy [the sinful kingdom] from the face of the earth,' the very next utterance is: 'Yet I will not totally destroy' (v. 8).

We come to the end of Amos with more than a glimmer of hope. Now, rather than destruction, the 'day' will bring restoration, repair, and rebuilding. Judgement will still happen, but there will be salvation. The imagery of the fruit returns, but this time the fruit is 'new wine' which will 'drip from the mountains and flow from all the hills' (v. 13). People will be brought back from exile, and they will do the work of rebuilding and restoring the broken and divided kingdom.

Amos has not held back in relaying all that he had heard from God. He had imparted the warnings he had been given in the form of judgements, sermons, and visions. He had been faithful to the Lord, yet the people did not listen to him.

Here, right at the end, God seems to change direction. Should we be surprised at this? No, it is in keeping with what we already know about God. God did not destroy the earth at the time of Noah; Nineveh was not destroyed at the time of Jonah; and God will not destroy Amos' Israel either. It is remarkable that, even though there was no sign of repentance, God still shows mercy. God had made a covenant with his people because God loves them, and because of this God will always give them hope and a second chance.

Thank you, Lord that you are merciful. Amen.

CLARE HAYNS

If you've enjoyed this set of reflections by **Clare Hayns**,
check out her books published with BRF Ministries, including...

Unveiled
Women of the Old Testament and the choices they made

978 1 80039 072 0
£14.99

Garden Song
Exploring the psalms through paintings, reflections and prayers

978 1 80039 068 3
£14.99

To order, visit **brfresources.org.uk** or use the order form at the end.

BRF Resources

Pausing to think, pray, and yield to God at every stage is a natural, vital element of the creative process. *Bless the Work of Our Hands* offers prayers, reflections, and biblical character studies to encourage Christian creatives to commit themselves and their projects to God. Written for hobbyists and paid professionals alike, playing and working in every genre, it encourages an honest, open-handed, and open-hearted approach, in order that all we produce and all we become from our creative toil may bring glory to God.

Bless the Work of Our Hands
Prayers and reflections for creatives
Written and illustrated by Jane Walters
978 1 80039 418 6 £12.99
brfresources.org.uk

Dementia is one of today's most feared health conditions, and Christians with the condition may also worry about losing their faith and their connection to God. However, there is still hope: those living with dementia can still find meaning in their life and their faith. Written by two practitioners in this field, Dementia, God and the Church aims to show how person-centred approaches to dementia can provide hope.

Dementia, God and the Church
Journeying with hope
Wendy Gleadle and Frances Attwood
978 1 80039 433 9 £12.99
brfresources.org.uk

SHARING OUR VISION – MAKING A GIFT

I would like to make a donation to support BRF Ministries.
Please use my gift for:

☐ Where the need is greatest ☐ Anna Chaplaincy ☐ BRF Resources
☐ Messy Church ☐ Parenting for Faith

Title	First name/initials	Surname

Address

Postcode

Email

Telephone

Signature | Date

Please accept my gift of:

☐ £2 ☐ £5 ☐ £10 ☐ £20 Other £ ______

by (*delete as appropriate*):

☐ Cheque/Charity Voucher payable to 'BRF'

☐ MasterCard/Visa/Debit card/Charity card

Name on card

Card no. ☐☐☐☐ ☐☐☐☐ ☐☐☐☐ ☐☐☐☐

Expires end M M Y Y

Signature | Date

Please complete the other side of the form ➔

BRF Ministries Gift Aid Declaration

In order to Gift Aid your donation, you must tick the box below.

☐ I want to Gift Aid my donation and any donation I make in the future or have made in the past four years to BRF Ministries

I am a UK taxpayer and understand that if I pay less Income Tax and/or Capital Gains Tax in the current tax year than the amount of Gift Aid claimed on all my donations, it is my responsibility to pay any difference.

Please notify BRF Ministries if you want to cancel this Gift Aid declaration, change your name or home address, or no longer pay sufficient tax on your income and/or capital gains.

You can also give online at **brf.org.uk/donate**, which reduces our administration costs, making your donation go further.

Our ministry is only possible because of the generous support of individuals, churches, trusts and gifts in wills.

☐ I would like to leave a gift to BRF Ministries in my will.
Please send me further information.

☐ I would like to find out about giving a regular gift to BRF Ministries.

For help or advice regarding making a gift, please contact our fundraising team +44 (0)1865 319700

Your privacy

We will use your personal data to process this transaction. From time to time we may send you information about the work of BRF Ministries that we think may be of interest to you. Our privacy policy is available at **brf.org.uk/privacy**. Please contact us if you wish to discuss your mailing preferences.

Registered with FUNDRAISING REGULATOR

Please complete the other side of the form

Please return this form to 'Freepost BRF'
No other address information or stamp is needed

Bible Reading Fellowship is a charity (233280) and company limited by guarantee (301324), registered in England and Wales

Overleaf... Reading *New Daylight* in a group | Author profile | Recommended reading | Order and subscription forms

Reading *New Daylight* in a group

GORDON GILES

St Benedict recommended daily scripture reading as a key aspect of the community life of work and prayer, and during Lent especially each monk was allocated a book to read daily. While Benedict's monks did not talk much, nowadays discussion and reflection can be helpful and enlightening when reading passages that others are reading simultaneously. Separated by space, as each reads alone, we are yet connected by the common food of scripture, taken in our own time, at our own pace. We each mull it over in our own way, and we can all learn from each other's insights and interpretations. Yet in Bible-reading fellowship with one another we are not alone and our thoughts, prayers, and reflections join with others worldwide. We bring our own stories and context to the mirror of scripture, to reflect mutually.

We can, of course, meet in groups together if the opportunity arises. To assist with that, here are some open questions to enable discussion in a Bible study or other group who gather to take further what is published here. The same questions may also aid personal devotion. Use them as you wish and may God bless and inspire you on your journey as you read, mark, and inwardly digest holy words to ponder and nourish the soul.

General discussion starters

These can be used for any study series within this issue. Remember there are no right or wrong answers – these questions are simply to enable a group to engage in conversation.

- What do you think is the main idea or theme of the author in this series? Did that come across strongly?
- Have any of the issues discussed touched on personal – or shared – aspects of your life?
- What evidence or stories do the authors draw on to illuminate, or be illuminated by, the passages of scripture.
- Which do you prefer: scripture informing daily modern life, or modern life shining a new light on scripture?
- Does the author 'call you to action' in a realistic and achievable way? Do you think their ideas will work in the secular world?

- Have any specific passages struck you personally? If so, how and why, do you think? Is God speaking to you through scripture and reflection?
- Was anything completely new to you? Any 'eureka' or jaw-dropping moments? If so, what difference will that make?

Questions for discussion

The game of faith: 1 and 2 Peter (Richard Martin)

- How helpful did you find the analogy of Peter as a sports coach?
- If you were writing a letter to your church, what would you say?
- Did any of these days' notes particularly strike you as relevant? Could you explain why?
- To what extent does having a Christian faith help a sports player? Can you think of any examples?

Abraham: Genesis 12—25 (Margaret Silf)

- How do you feel about 'patriarchy'? Does the story of Abraham change your feelings at all?
- Leaving the comfort zone, while always difficult, sometimes leads us to a place of new growth. Has this ever been your own experience?
- In the relationship between Abraham and Lot, excessive possessions lead to conflict. Is this a pattern that you recognise?
- Abraham's story includes the very destructive experience of being an alien or refugee without a name, language, or status. How does this ancient story connect for you with events in our own time and place?
- The presentation of Sarai/Sarah in the story is quite negative. To what extent is this justified? Could it be characterised as misogynistic?
- How do you view the parallels between the stories of Isaac and Ishmael? Is it right to understand contemporary relationships between modern nations as rooted in this story?

Mountains and hills (Barbara Mosse)

- How do we expect to encounter God? Are we prepared to have our expectations challenged?
- 'Moses drew near to the thick darkness where God was' (Exodus 20:21, NRSV). How comfortable are you with the image of God living in 'thick darkness'?
- Peter's response to the transfiguration experience was to offer to set up tents for Jesus, Moses, and Elijah. Why was this not appropriate?
- Humanly, we find it impossible to grasp the time spans involved from the dawn of creation to God's final consummation of all things. How helpful do you find the imagery used in Psalm 90?
- Why might Jesus have chosen a mountain to deliver his famous sermon on the mount (Matthew 5)?
- How do we encounter Christ in the everyday, apart from mountaintop experiences?

Exodus 1—4 (David Walker)

- Moses and the Israelites are both a feared and an oppressed minority in Egypt. What can we learn from their story with regard to how migrant communities are treated in our own country today? Is there a role your group or church can play?
- Moses turned aside to inspect the burning bush. Where can we see signs of God, miraculous or otherwise, in our own communities and places today? Is there something your group or church can join in with?
- The land Moses leads the Israelites back to, the land where they had formerly lived, was already settled by others. Is there any part we can play, as Christians and churches, in situations where territory remains disputed to this day?
- Pharaoh and the Egyptians were condemned and punished severely by God for refusing to let the Israelites go free. Some of us studying these passages will be descended from those enslaved when European nations colonised Africa. Some of us may worship in churches built by the proceeds of slavery.

Is slavery simply a forgiven sin of the past or are there ways in which we should respond to its legacy today?

- Moses feels inadequate to the calling God has given him, so God includes Aaron in that call. When have we felt not up to the task, and where can we see how God has found others to work with us? Where do we need help today?
- God both hardens the heart of Pharaoh and then punishes the Egyptians for their resistance. How do we interpret such difficult passages in the Bible, in the light of both the wider themes of the Hebrew scriptures and of the New Testament?

Amos (Clare Hayns)

- Where do we see examples today of people practising outward religion while ignoring issues of justice and compassion? How can faith communities remain authentic and action-driven?
- How can we speak out against injustice, just as Amos did, in a world where doing so can be risky or unpopular? What qualities help someone stand firm when facing opposition?
- In what ways have wealth and comfort today led to complacency or indifference to the suffering of others? How might media, social media, or materialism distract us from engaging with real-world problems.
- How might prayer and intercession, like Amos' pleas for mercy, make a real difference in situations of global or local crisis today? Can you think of examples where prayer movements or spiritual leadership have had an impact on situations like wars, natural disasters, or injustice.
- What are some modern examples of 'the poor being trampled' or 'justice being denied' that Amos condemned? What practical actions align with Amos' call for justice?
- If 'justice rolling like a river' means deep, lasting societal change, what steps can individuals and communities take today to help that happen? Brainstorm small and big actions – from voting and volunteering to policymaking and advocacy work.

Meet the author: Clare Hayns

Where do you live and what does your current ministry involve?
I am currently the vicar of St Mary's Church, a beautiful 12th-century church in Iffley, Oxford – people come from far and wide to see the building, but it is also a vibrant parish church. Before this I was college chaplain and welfare coordinator at Christ Church, Oxford. My background is in social work, where I worked for some years with homeless young people and with a drug and alcohol service in London. When my three children were young, I left social work to set up an entertainment agency with my husband John, who is a magician.

Tell us about some of your other writing.
A few years ago, I set myself the challenge of creating a Lent blog writing on 40 women of the Old Testament. This led to the creation of *Unveiled: Women of the Old Testament and the choices they made*, a book with my artist son Micah Hayns, published by BRF Ministries. We then followed up with a book on the psalms, *Garden Song*. We love travelling around the country to speak to church groups on our books, with Micah often leading art workshops.

What inspires you about the Bible?
I love relating the Bible to life today and telling rarely told stories – my favourite is the story of the five daughters of Zelophehad, plucky women who changed Moses' mind and transformed land rights for women (Numbers 27). I get frustrated when these women's stories get missed out of the lectionary and are so rarely preached on in church.

What do you like to do in your spare time?
I enjoy running and challenge myself to do a half-marathon once a year. I volunteer with Musical Youth Company, Oxford, and love seeing young people flourish on stage. I have three sons, a couple of pets, and like nothing more than playing a board game with good friends and family. I also love going to see a good musical.

Recommended reading

A biblical exposition with testimonies of contemporary migration. In *Come for Refuge*, Pete Wilcox, Bishop of Sheffield, invites you to read the book of Ruth through the lens of the present global migration crisis. By interweaving an exposition of the text of Ruth with testimonies from contemporary migrants, creating a conversation between the two, this book offers a hopeful vision of what migration can contribute to the world. An essential study guide for individuals and churches.

The following is an edited extract taken from the introduction.

The book of Ruth is the story not just of one woman, but of two: Ruth and Naomi. The whole narrative is only four chapters long: Naomi is most prominent in chapters 1 and 4 (though Ruth is present), and Ruth is most prominent in chapters 2 and 3 (though Naomi is present). Both women had experience of migration: Naomi was an Israelite who went to live as a migrant in the land of Moab; Ruth was a Moabite who went to live as a migrant in the land of Israel. For Naomi, migration was essentially a bitter experience; for Ruth, a much more fulfilling one – she sought and found refuge (the word is used of her in 2:12) in Bethlehem and almost certainly never returned to her country of origin.

This exposition of the book of Ruth seeks to pay particular attention to those experiences of migration. I would argue that the text invites this focus, not least by the way in which it repeatedly places stress on Ruth's migrant status: again and again, sometimes gratuitously, she is described as 'Ruth the Moabite' and once she is described as 'the Moabite… from the country of Moab' (2:6). Once she describes herself as 'a foreigner' (2:10) – in Hebrew, *nākerîyāh*, an alien.

However, my sensitivity to this emphasis in the book of Ruth has been heightened by my recent interactions with migrants and refugees in the two cities in the UK in which I have lived in the past twelve years: specifically with refugees and asylum seekers from Iran, Kurdistan, and Ukraine. Their stories of leaving a beloved homeland, of risk-laden journeys, of uncertain and uneven welcomes in a new and deeply unfamiliar country have enriched (among other things) my reading of this biblical text.

That enrichment is what has prompted me to experiment with the format in this book. I have tried to create a conversation between the experience of Ruth and Naomi, on the one hand, and that of some contemporary migrants, refugees, and asylum seekers, on the other. I am deeply grateful to those individuals who have confided their stories in me and who have trusted me to place their testimonies alongside the Bible story. How far this experiment is a success will be for others to judge, but I am immensely grateful to those whose risky frankness with me made the experiment possible. I am especially thankful to those who provided me with testimonies which, on account of various inevitable editorial considerations, I have not ultimately been able to include in this book. Their generosity, patience, grace, and understanding have been exemplary.

These testimonies are drawn from two contexts: Sheffield, in England, where I serve as bishop of the Anglican Diocese, and Melbourne, Australia, where I drafted much of this book during a period of sabbatical leave.

As the bishop of Sheffield, it is my privilege to be one of the patrons of a magnificent charity called ASSIST, which seeks to support some of the most vulnerable people in our City of Sanctuary. So it was an obvious step, not least as a way of drawing attention to the extraordinary work of the staff and volunteers of ASSIST, to seek to secure some of these testimonies from among those the charity has supported – though not all the 'Sheffield' stories are 'ASSIST' stories.

Part of the point of this book is to underline that migration is a global challenge requiring a global response. Our experience of increased migration to the UK in recent decades is by no means unique – quite the opposite. On sabbatical, I had barely been in Melbourne for 48 hours before I became aware of the extent of migration to that city at present and of the work of the Anglican Church in seeking to support asylum seekers, refugees, and other migrants there. The opportunity to include testimonies from migrants to Melbourne seemed, in the providence of God, too good to miss; and I am delighted that it has proved possible.

To order a copy of this book, please use the order form or visit ***brfresources.org.uk****.*

To order

Online: **brfresources.org.uk**
Telephone: +44 (0)1865 319700
Mon–Fri 9.30–17.00

Delivery times within the UK are normally 15 working days. Prices are correct at the time of going to press but may change without prior notice.

Title	Price	Qty	Total
Bless the Work of Our Hands	£12.99		
Unveiled	£14.99		
Garden Song	£14.99		
Dementia, God and the Church	£12.99		
Come for Refuge	£9.99		
Belonging without Barriers	£14.99		

POSTAGE AND PACKING CHARGES			
Order value	UK	Europe	Rest of world
Under £7.00	£2.00	Available on request	Available on request
£7.00–£29.99	£3.00		
£30.00 and over	FREE		

Total value of books	
Postage and packing	
Donation*	
Total for this order	

* Please complete and return the Gift Aid declaration on page 144.

Please complete in BLOCK CAPITALS

Title .... First name/initials .... Surname ....

Address ....

.... Postcode ....

Acc. No. .... Telephone ....

Email ....

Method of payment

❑ Cheque (made payable to BRF) ❑ MasterCard / Visa

Card no. ☐☐☐☐ ☐☐☐☐ ☐☐☐☐ ☐☐☐☐

Expires end M M Y Y

We will use your personal data to process this order. From time to time we may send you information about the work of BRF Ministries. Please contact us if you wish to discuss your mailing preferences. Our privacy policy is available at **brf.org.uk/privacy**.

Please return this form to:

BRF Ministries, 15 The Chambers, Vineyard, Abingdon OX14 3FE | **enquiries@brf.org.uk**

For terms and cancellation information, please visit **brfresources.org.uk/terms**.

BRF Ministries needs you!

If you're one of our many thousands of regular *New Daylight* readers, you will know all about the benefits and blessings of regular Bible reading and the value of daily notes to guide, inform, and inspire you.

Here are some recent comments from *New Daylight* readers:

'Thank you for all the many inspiring writings that help so much when things are tough.'

'Just right for me – I learned a lot!'

'We looked forward to each day's message as we pondered each passage and comment.'

If you have similarly positive things to say about *New Daylight*, would you be willing to share your experience with others? Could you ask for a brief slot during church notices or write a short piece for your church magazine or website? Do you belong to groups, formal or informal, where you could share your experience of using Bible reading notes and encourage others to try them?

It doesn't need to be complicated or nerve-wracking: just answering these three questions in what you say or write will get your message across:

- How do Bible reading notes help you grow in your faith?
- Where, when and how do you use them?
- What would you say to people who don't already use them?

We can supply further information if you need it and and would love to hear about it if you do find ways to get *New Daylight* into new readers' hands.

For more information:

- Email **enquiries@brf.org.uk**
- Phone us on **+44 (0)1865 319700** Mon–Fri 9.30–17.00
- Write to us at BRF Ministries, 15 The Chambers, Vineyard, Abingdon OX14 3FE

Inspiring people of all ages to grow in Christian faith

At BRF Ministries, we long for people of all ages to grow in faith and understanding of the Bible. That's what all our work as a charity is about.

- Our range of **BRF Resources** helps Christians go deeper in their understanding of scripture, in prayer and in their walk with God. Our conferences and events bring people together to share this journey, while our Holy Habits resources help whole congregations grow together as disciples of Jesus, living out and sharing their faith.
- We also want to make it easier for local churches to engage effectively in ministry and mission – by helping them bring new families into a growing relationship with God through **Messy Church** or by supporting churches as they nurture the spiritual life of older people through **Anna Chaplaincy**.
- Our **Parenting for Faith** team coaches parents and others to raise God-connected children and teens, and enables churches to fully support them.

Do you share our vision?

Though a significant proportion of BRF Ministries' funding is generated through our charitable activities, we are dependent on the generous support of individuals, churches and charitable trusts.

If you share our vision, would you help us to enable even more people of all ages to grow in faith? Your prayers and financial support are vital for the work that we do. You could:

- support us with a regular donation or one-off gift
- consider leaving a gift to BRF Ministries in your will
- encourage your church to support us as part of your church's giving to home mission – perhaps focusing on a specific ministry or programme
- most important of all, support us with your prayers.

Donate at **brf.org.uk/donate** or use the form on pages 143–44.

Bearing fruit

'Remain in me, as I also remain in you. No branch can bear fruit by itself; it must remain in the vine. Neither can you bear fruit unless you remain in me.'

JOHN 15:4 (NIV)

As a charity, BRF Ministries is always doing a huge assortment of things, from our Anna Chaplaincy team equipping people to minister to older people to our Messy Church team bringing Jesus to families across the world. From our Parenting for Faith ministry reaching parents and church leaders to transform ideas about how to raise God-connected children to our BRF Resources, which span so many different topics to help people to develop their faith journey.

At a glance these activities might seem distant or disparate, but a closer look shows the vine from which all our ministries grow – the mission set out by Leslie Mannering over 100 years ago, to which we still hold today: inspiring people of all ages to grow in Christian faith. God is at the heart of all that we do, and we are hugely thankful for all the fruit we have born through these works over the last century and more.

We want to keep building on this work, adapting, growing and finding even more glorious ways for people to grow in their faith while still remaining rooted to our mission.

This work would not be possible without kind donations from individuals, charitable trusts and gifts in wills. If you would like to support us now and in the future, you can become a Friend of BRF Ministries by making a monthly gift of £2 or more. We thank you for your friendship.

Find out more at **brf.org.uk/donate** or get in touch with us on **+44 (0)1865 319700** or via **giving@brf.org.uk**.

We thank you for your support and your prayers.

The fundraising team at BRF Ministries

Give. Pray. Get involved.
brf.org.uk

NEW DAYLIGHT SUBSCRIPTION RATES

Please note our new subscription rates, current until 30 April 2027:

Individual subscriptions
covering three issues for under six copies, payable in advance (including postage and packing):

	UK	**Europe**	**Rest of world**
New Daylight	£25.50	£37.50	£44.25
New Daylight Deluxe per set of 3 issues p.a.	£30.15	£45.15	£61.05

Copies may also be obtained from Christian bookshops:

New Daylight	£5.99 per copy
New Daylight Deluxe	£7.25 per copy

All our Bible reading notes can be ordered online by visiting
brfresources.org.uk/subscriptions

NEW DAYLIGHT SUBSCRIPTION FORM

To set up a recurring subscription, please go to
brfresources.org.uk/subscriptions

Title .... First name/initials .... Surname ....

Address ....

.... Postcode ....

Telephone .... Email ....

Please send ***New Daylight*** beginning with the September 2026 / January 2027 / May 2027 issue (*delete as appropriate*):

(*please tick box*)	UK	Europe	Rest of world
New Daylight	☐ £25.50	☐ £37.50	☐ £44.25
New Daylight Deluxe	☐ £30.15	☐ £45.15	☐ £61.05

Optional donation to support the work of BRF Ministries £ ....

Total enclosed £ .... (cheques should be made payable to 'BRF')

Please complete and return the Gift Aid declaration on page 144 to make your donation even more valuable to us.

Please charge my MasterCard / Visa with £ ....

Card no. ☐☐☐☐ ☐☐☐☐ ☐☐☐☐ ☐☐☐☐

Expires end M M Y Y

We will use your personal data to process this order. From time to time we may send you information about the work of BRF Ministries. Please contact us if you wish to discuss your mailing preferences. Our privacy policy is available at **brf.org.uk/privacy**.

Please return this form with the appropriate payment to:
BRF Ministries, 15 The Chambers, Vineyard, Abingdon OX14 3FE
For terms and cancellation information, please visit **brfresources.org.uk/terms**.

Bible Reading Fellowship is a charity (233280) and company limited by guarantee (301324), registered in England and Wales

Enjoy a little luxury: upgrade to *New Daylight deluxe*

Many readers enjoy the compact format of the regular *New Daylight* but more and more people are discovering the advantages of the larger format, premium edition, *New Daylight deluxe.* The pocket-sized version is perfect if you're reading on the move but the larger print, white paper and extra space to write your own notes and comments all make the deluxe edition an attractive alternative and significant upgrade.

Why not try it to see if you like it? You can order single copies at brfresources.org.uk/newdaylightdeluxe

Deluxe actual size:

gladness instead of mourning, the mantle of
spirit. They will be called oaks of righteousness,
to display his glory.

We learn from these verses that gladness is first
them' gladness instead of mourning and praise in
gift needs to be received, and action is often re
gift. For example, receiving a piano is of little us
play it. God has blessed us with 'every spiritual
but, metaphorically speaking, *we* have to pour o
put on and wear the mantle of praise. The Lord